TRADITIONAL ROMANCE AND TALE

TRADITIONAL ROMANCE AND TALE

How Stories Mean

ANNE WILSON

D. S. BREWER · ROWMAN & LITTLEFIELD

Published by D. S. Brewer Ltd.,
P.O. Box 24 Ipswich IP1 1JJ

ISBN 0 85991
US edition ISBN 0 87471 905 4

*Dedicated to
my husband
and
children*

The author's thanks are due to the proprietors of the copyrights in the following works quoted in the text: *Grimm's Fairy Tales*, translated by Edgar Taylor (Oxford University Press). *Grimm's Fairy Tales*, translated by Margaret Hunt and thoroughly revised, corrected and completed by James Stern (Routledge & Kegan Paul Ltd). *Homer: The Odyssey*, translated by E. V. Rieu; *Sir Gawain and the Green Knight*, translated by Brian Stone (Penguin Books Ltd). *Alice's Adventures in Wonderland and Through the Looking-Glass*, by Lewis Carroll (Macmillan). *Art and Tradition in Sir Gawain and the Green Knight*, by Larry D. Benson (Rutgers University Press).

Filmset in Monophoto 10 on 11 pt. Times by
Richard Clay (The Chaucer Press), Ltd., Bungay, Suffolk
and printed in Great Britain by
Fletcher & Son Ltd., Norwich

Contents

1 Story as Festival   1

2 Story as Dream   9

3 Story and Fantasy   20

4 Disguises   34

5 Form   55

6 Imagery   72

7 Transformation and Recognition   84

8 Sir Gawain and the Green Knight   96

  Conclusion   109

  Select Bibliography   111

  Index   116

Preface

THIS BOOK SUGGESTS a completely new approach to the study of traditional literature, which includes medieval romance and folk-tale. It argues the case for this approach, and demonstrates it with detailed discussion of particular stories.

It first asks why these stories, which lack everyday logic, have proved so popular that they were transmitted faithfully in every detail through oral tradition, and have survived for centuries subsequently. Hitherto, no approaches to medieval romance or folktale have taken this into account. Those who trace the stories back to ancient rituals, customs or 'events', or even to earlier versions, are not explaining why the stories remained so popular among the unscholarly. Nor does an approach which isolates particular features explain why each story is appreciated in its entirety.

This book suggests that if the story-telling experience is one of creation and recreation on the part of the story-teller and his audience, and if identification with the protagonist of the story does take place, then the story-teller, the audience and the protagonist should be seen as united. The approach argues that each story should be viewed as its protagonist's creation.

The book then tests this theory, in the case of *Sir Gawain and the Green Knight*, *Tristan*, *King Horn*, and other medieval romances. It also looks at *The Odyssey* and some folktales.

We cannot immediately see these stories as making sense by taking up the point of view suggested, because the thinking in them is not predominantly the kind of thinking which we bring to our everyday affairs, or expect to find in novels. The thinking of stories is apparently dreamlike: there is an exploration of their pictorial and magical nature, together with the disguises employed. In order to keep the discussion clear and coherent, there are some tentative attempts at interpretation, but the study insists that, as stories are deeply complex and carry multiple meaning, any interpretation can only be controversial. This book is a study of the nature of stories—how they mean—rather than what they mean.

Essentially, this is a literary study, and any psychological or psychoanalytic elements are subordinated to the study of the stories as artistic entities. No specialist language is employed.

Such an exploration of the nature of stories arose quite unexpectedly, while I was studying the medieval romances as festival literature. I was deeply struck by the strangeness of the stories, and began to ask why they had come into existence, how their apparently crazy events could have been faithfully transmitted in the oral tradition, and why they still make such a powerful impression upon us.

At first, I did not know how to approach the romances in such a way that I could see each one as making some kind of sense as a whole. My early work was much held up by presuppositions and analogy, and by a failure to take upon myself certain disciplines which I later realized are essential. My first step forward was my realization that I must approach each story with my mind empty of everything else—as do listeners. Then came what I regard as my major step forward: my realization that identification is likely to be the key to meaning in story. If the story-teller, and we ourselves, become Tristan as we follow that particular romance, then the story should technically be seen as created by Tristan, who represents the people who create and recreate the story. The characters and events of the romance, including the way Tristan himself appears in it, should be viewed as figments of the hero's mind.

I began to test this theory by joining the protagonist of each romance in turn, putting all other romances firmly out of my mind, and dwelling on the romance for several weeks or months. At first each romance appeared unfathomable to me, and my task proved long and hard. I had to begin each study by experiencing the story feelingly and imaginatively, and then I had to study these experiences analytically. Contemplating such features as the three Isoldes in *Tristan*, and the strange character 'Dwarf Tristan', I realized that the romances are more like dreams than I had previously suspected, in that their fundamental language seems to be pictorial, magical and disguised. I was also aware that there are differences, in that, as works of art, stories have decided form and a number of other characteristics which appeal to the conscious mind. However, of nothing—not even of my chosen standpoint from which to view each romance—could there be any kind of certainty until I had made some sense of this enormously difficult dreamlike thinking which appeared to be the nature of the hero's thought-processes.

At this stage, I decided to abandon my previous research, and make this exhausting and maybe impossible task my PhD work. I was certain that the seemingly crazy romances did each of them have a logic of some kind, and I hoped that I might be able to discern enough of it to establish that the standpoint from which we should view the stories is in the mind of the protagonist. The task stretched every aspect of my mind to its limits. I had had a little experience of dream-analysis, but not really enough to make the puzzling language of the romances more than vaguely familiar in places, and the fact that nearly all the romances are 'hero' stories, not 'heroine' ones, did not make them any easier to me. Moreover, as I dwelt on each story, I realized that they were expressing many things at once, while some images—like that of the Loathly Lady—remained wholly inscrutable for two years. So enormous and confusing was my task that my work was often held up by failure in discipline. I was tempted, for instance, to discount unfathomable details, even though I knew that every detail was vitally important and that if I could not somehow give a coherent explanation for the presence of every detail in the sequence of the story, my theory would have to be abandoned.

At a vital stage, I was greatly helped by my reading of Vladimir Propp's study, *Morphology of the Folktale*, for it liberated me from the trammels of detail in such a way that I was able to embark on a fruitful examination of the form of each romance. After applying Propp's theories to my own for some months, I began to discern a pattern of repetition in each romance—a pattern outstandingly clear in *King Horn* and the earlier parts of *Clariodus*. Two of my children then had dreams which, I realized, could be of value to my study, since one showed the repetition pattern and the other had a beheading incident, which is a puzzling and frequent incident in medieval romance.

However, another factor was now coming to the fore which caused me considerable concern: this related to the nature of the 'sense' which seemed to be emerging in each romance. All the romances appear to contain material which is 'disturbing' in some way, especially those which are better known and which therefore would lend themselves better to my discussion. I was also disappointed to find that, while each romance is indeed unique in that the significance of every element depends entirely on its particular context within its particular romance, the thoughts which seem to frame the unifying logic of each story were emerging as extraordinarily similar. Studying each romance in terms of itself, strictly avoiding any analogy—which could only be wholly misleading—I found myself involved in subject-matter which was apparently violent and frightening, and that hate, incest, patricide and other such concerns, appeared to be present. The disguises which I had observed were clearly there for a good reason, even if I was making mistakes in my tentative and increasingly reluctant interpretation. I knew that such disguises should not be removed, and yet I also knew that I would never produce a case for my thesis if I did not remove them. While people in general would naturally prefer to leave the disguises of stories untouched, since their enjoyment of stories would thus be the greater, it is the business of literary scholars to seek to understand the nature of literary creations. Perhaps stories have a particular rôle in our communal life, being a means by which we may share feelings of which we do not approve: feelings of which we approve have many outlets and need no disguise.

I wished that it was not necessary to produce any interpretations, and it was anyway now obvious that the matters of the recommended viewpoint and the dreamlike thinking, which I was discussing, were much more interesting and important. Attempts at interpretation could, at best, only present a timeless work of art in terms of something much smaller than itself, and it might give rise to a prejudice, or to some other kind of emotional reaction, which might divert attention from the main point of this study. I therefore decided to include direct interpretation in my discussion only where it was essential for the clarity of the argument. For this present version of my research, in which folktales and *The Odyssey* have replaced many of the medieval romances, every attempt has been made to find stories which combine the qualities of being adequately known, substantial enough to be the subject of study and lacking in disturbing subject-matter—with little success. I also had to keep other considerations in mind as I selected stories from the great number which I have studied. No study of stories should leave out *Tristan*, *Sir Gawain and the Green Knight* or *The Odyssey*, and since only a few stories can be discussed, those which show a number of important features in a short space are obvious choices. 'Heroine' stories must appear alongside 'hero' ones, although, alas, there are fewer of note, and I lack space for the discussion of slighter stories. In the end, saddened that I would probably offend many people, I determined on completing what I believed to be an important task in literary scholarship to the best of my ability.

Another serious problem associated with interpretation is the very fact that every incident in a story appears to mean many things at once. In this study, I use the word 'mean' to refer to that which the creator of the story purposefully has in mind, to that which he is thinking about with sustained intent. In my first analyses of the romances, each incident took up pages of discussion. This work was invaluable to me in my exploration as to how stories mean: I studied the activity of the many processes of thought involved—magical thinking, the working of the defences, the crystallization of feelings into images, and the activity of the intellect as it plays its part in the artistic organization of the story. This was the main interest of my study, but readers found that it made confusing and slow reading; and obscured, rather than clarified, my central argument. Thus I had another reason for reducing my discussion of meaning to a minimum—but, once again, some interpretation was necessary to make my discussion of the mental processes apparently at work in story sufficiently clear. It is particularly unfortunate that the inclusion of some interpretation has proved necessary while it is quite impracticable to attempt an exploration of all that a story means, because this can direct attention away from the essentially complex nature of stories.

A further problem associated with the decision to omit full interpretative discussion, is that this does not help me to prove that every story is consistently intelligible in every detail. It is hoped that the remaining discussion is full enough to show the validity of this important aspect of my argument.

Several other points must be mentioned. I have given great attention to the labours of others in the field of stories, but, unfortunately, my discussion of their remarkable work has had to be cut in this abbreviated version of my research, along with much other material. Publication costs have made this necessary. I must also make clear that the subjects of study in this book are traditional stories only—those originating from communal, oral tradition. The individual works of authors, from those of Hans Andersen to those of novelists, are not my concern. It is extremely unlikely that my work applies at all to the greatest achievements of the novelists, where a conscious, intellectual control governs the entire imaginative creation. However, there is a possibility that it may have some limited value in the study of novels: in *Jane Eyre*, for instance, both the 'moves' of a romance and the realism of a novel may be discerned. I am planning to do some research in this field. At this point I must say that, while my present research has led to my appreciating all the more the transcending achievements of our great writers, it has also deepened my respect for traditional stories as works of art, and my wonder at the variety and quality of our powers of mind.

My greatest debt is to my husband, Anthony Wilson, and to my children, Kenneth, Frances and Martin. My husband's critical scrutiny and practical suggestions have given me invaluable help with the presentation of the discussion. Kenneth helped me when I was wholly puzzled by the significance of the Green Knight's colour, and Frances asked the all-important question about the Sleeping Beauty's strangely negligent parents. Adult minds are constantly hampered by habits of thinking which hinder direct response and the conception of essential questions.

Professor G. T. Shepherd, of the University of Birmingham, supervised my research, and it was extremely fortunate that, after having been absent from the academic world for about fifteen years (living in Central Africa), I should have had the help of a supervisor who combined stringent criticism with generous help. It was he who suggested that I study the romances, in an attempt to discover what it is in them that catches the mind, and his wide scholarship ensured that I read important books from a great variety of areas of research. I am also extremely grateful to Dr D. S. Brewer, of Emmanuel College, Cambridge, and to Mrs Elisabeth Brewer, for all the help and encouragement which they have given me in turning my thesis into a book.

While scarcely knowing the nature of my study—since I scarcely knew it myself for so long—many friends and relatives have given valuable help. I must mention particularly Mrs L. Agnes Finnegan, whose insights into stories were invaluable to me during the most difficult period of my study, and Professor Dorothy Emmet, who read the MS. of my thesis and gave me much help and encouragement. I must also mention Mr Thomas Braun of Merton College, Oxford, who gave me valuable help with the proper names in *The Odyssey*. My deep gratitude goes also to Dr G. Hope Scott, without whose profound knowledge and perception this work would not have been possible.

Finally, I wish to remember the English Department of Manchester University in the fifties, where, as Anne Brockington and the student primarily of Dr Ida L. Gordon, I first came to love medieval literature.

Anne D. Wilson
Birmingham, 1976

1   Story as Festival

WHY DID THE parents of the Sleeping Beauty not remember that she was to be pricked by a spinning-wheel upon reaching her fifteenth birthday? Why did they not look in their diaries, had they not, for some strange reason, felt a continual anxiety which would have kept the approaching disaster constantly in their minds? Equally, we might ask of *Sir Gawain and the Green Knight*, how could there be a green knight? Why does he suggest such an extraordinary game? How could he survive his beheading, especially as he later turns out to be mortal? How could Sir Gawain find him again to keep their appointment, without any directions whatever? Why do Sir Gawain and his aunt remain in ignorance of their relationship throughout Christmas at Sir Bercilak's castle? What is all this magic?

If we bring to such stories the logic which we apply to our everyday affairs, we find them completely ridiculous, and yet, while we may ask these questions, the strangeness and illogicality of the stories does not really worry us. Why not? The answer must be that we are not looking for this kind of logic. In that case, what logic are we looking for? Indeed, what coherent sense do we perceive?—for we clearly do perceive some. Otherwise, we surely could not have loved these seemingly ridiculous forms of art as we have long done, and preserved them, passing them faithfully down the generations. What is it that catches our minds?

This book will be a quest for the answers to these questions. It will not seek to establish precisely what stories mean: its aim will be to discover how we should approach stories in order to see meaning in them. Moreover, it will explore the ways in which we should be thinking, as we study stories, in order to apprehend their meaning.

Many scholars regard stories as memories of the past; as, to a great extent, remnants of ancient custom and ritual, or earlier stories.[1] Consigning the beheading idea in *Sir Gawain and the Green Knight* to such origins, one scholar then writes:

> If the Gawain-poet or his audience thought about such matters at all, they probably would have connected the beheading in *Sir Gawain* with the 'exchange of blows', for that primitive tale was still current in English romance.[2]

1

Another approach to stories is the somewhat piecemeal one of studying isolated incidents. This is often accompanied by the comparison approach, identifying recurrent incidents. Thus we have 'the Beheading Game' or 'Challenge', 'the Fairy Mistress story', 'the Captive Maiden', 'the Enchanted Princess', 'the Two Brothers', 'the Faithful Servitor', 'the Grateful Beast', and so forth.[3] Another feature discernable in studies of stories is the symbolizing approach, which treats the elements of stories as symbols. Only too often, care is not taken to study the elements concerned in their contexts, and the symbolizers bring to their study ideas which apparently originate from somewhere outside the text. Their work is also often damaged by preconceptions and analogy. For example, John Speirs interprets the young woman in *Sir Gawain and the Green Knight* as the new year, and the old woman as the old year.[4] But anyone who has entered into the story and experienced it imaginatively, experiences the young woman as essentially a woman, with sexual power, and the old woman as also a woman, with sinister power. Is there anything witchlike about an old year?

While there has been much interesting and important work done on stories, it has not been dealing with them directly on their own terms. Above all, this work does not take into account the full implications of the fact that these stories arose and survived as an art form in a popular tradition, first of all oral,[5] and then literary. It might be best to begin any study of a story by telling it to an audience. Anyone telling the story of *Sir Gawain and the Green Knight* will find that audiences certainly do think about such matters as beheading, and that they do so for reasons quite other than that they have heard such themes recounted in stories before. An audience which has never heard of the 'sources and analogues' of the story, and knows nothing of ancient rituals, becomes greatly excited by the Green Knight's beheading game. The story appears to have immediate importance to them personally. It appears, moreover, to capture the minds of audiences when presented in language other than that in which the great Gawain-poet recreated it. It seems clear that stories have an appeal which transcends the skill of any individual story-teller.

A striking factor in the oral and literary traditions is the faithfulness of the transmission. Alterations may take place, but the manifest tendency has been to transmit stories with astonishingly few alterations to the characters and incidents in the story. Where there are apparent alterations, they are rarely found, upon analysis of the story, to have changed its themes. Alterations in detail, and also the processes of simplification and elaboration, remain faithful to the story. The many versions of folktales provide good examples of this, but further discussion on this point would be more satisfactory later in this study.[6] Suffice it to say now that even minute elements are usually remembered. Our own experience of story-telling reinforces the shadowy evidence of our past oral tradition. Listeners will correct the story-teller when they feel that he has altered any small details. How can this happen unless the details are felt to be of vital importance?

The meaning in story which we should be seeking must therefore involve every detail. It is not enough to point out the presence of themes (albeit they may certainly be present and important to the story) if they do not explain the presence of every element of the story. Furthermore, the explanations which we should be seeking will not be vague ones. Only decided meaning will impinge upon the memory of the listener and transmitter. Images such as a beheading ogre, a 'perilous chapel', a bestial future husband or a beautiful witch, are vividly conceived by both story-teller and audience, and, therefore, studies of story must be cautious about dismissing any images as being present in the story for only casual, idle reasons, or as being comprehensible only to those with recourse to scholarship. All those who love a story find it meaningful and, in order to grasp this meaning, we must be as faithful to the story as the listeners and transmitters have been. We must take upon our-selves a discipline which rules out preconceptions, and analogy with other stories which we know. A listener to a story—as opposed to someone whose mind is not captured—thinks only of the story as he listens; he enters into the world of the story and is momentarily concerned with nothing outside it. We must also do this, in order to see why it is that the particular story is, in its entirety and its every part, of such importance to the listener that it is, in its complete form, firmly implanted in his memory.

The story as it is now, enjoyed by people now, is the concern of this study, and it must begin with the story itself and not with theories[7] about it, which rarely interest those who enjoy the story.

A work of art is what it does to us. Even if we read *Sir Gawain and the Green Knight* alone it is never just the print on the page. It is what happens between the creator and those at the other end of the bridge which he has built between his inner world and theirs. The African literary critic, Cosmo Pieterse, has described African poetry, in a lecture, as not just a thing of words: it enters into the psyche of the audience and is a happening. It is essentially a com-munal poem. Music, dance, singing and ritual become one vast ceremony: the poem. The dance is not just entertainment; it is also functional and communal. The chant of language pinpoints the ritual of performance. It refers to all time, not just now, and it stretches from feast to nightmare.[8] Cosmo Pieterse was recalling literature as an oral and ritual experience. It is a special activity,

3

quite distinct from the experience of reading a story alone. The story-teller and the audience are both active, and the story grows as the audience participates and responds. Its creation takes place at that very time, born of that particular circle, however old its themes, and the words and phrases used to convey them, may be. Indeed, the repetition of the themes and elements of a story, of the formulae of language and the individual words themselves, is one of the delights of story. Reading any version of *Little Red Riding-Hood*, we can still sense through the written words, the oral story as it was passed down through the ages, chanted as if it were a rite. The words, known by heart, will only have varied slightly with each telling. They led each audience on through each well-known and well-beloved incident, until the crescendo was reached:

> ' "Oh grandmother, what big teeth you have!"
> "All the better to eat you with, my dear!" '

The words vary slightly in English versions, and naturally they are different in the versions of Charles Perrault and the Brothers Grimm, but their purport is exactly the same. In the oral situation, the members of the audience will correct the teller, if they consider that he has diverged unsatisfactorily from either the chanted words which they love, or from the progression of events.

Observation of groups in which a story is being told reveals that they are essentially dynamic. Everyone is deeply involved.[9] During the time of the telling of the story, the story is being recreated in the mind of each member of the company. This could not happen if it were not deeply significant and important. It is indeed felt to be deeply significant and important at the time of its telling—although the company may laugh at it later and call it ridiculous and senseless. 'It was only about a little girl and a wolf', they might say. But they will remember their absorption in the story and perhaps wonder at it. When asked why they enjoyed it, they might laugh and give no reason, their attitude being that it was nonsense but fun. True nonsense, however, a truly meaningless collection of characters and events, would be experienced as totally boring. Stories of this kind could never come into being or be transmitted. The wholly meaningless cannot appeal to the mind in any way; it is instantly forgotten. The 'nonsense' which we enjoy only appears as nonsense to part of our minds. One of the particular delights of story is that we experience in the phenomenon both the puzzling and the profoundly meaningful at one and the same time. The latter response is our predominant one, provided that we are not asked for an 'explanation', and it does not normally occur to anyone to ask for any explanation in depth. It is usually assumed that there cannot be one, and if we try to

4

explain a story, we quickly become puzzled, confused and ready to discount it altogether.

Thus it comes about that we both create and enjoy stories, while having little idea why we do so. Nevertheless, we do like to think that we know why we enjoy stories, and will therefore find facile explanations for both their existence and their subject-matter. Where the latter is concerned, it is important to note that successful art can always be given some superficial interpretation. Indeed, all the arts must be comprehensible at some superficial level in order to have success. Our intellect desires the satisfaction of perceiving some kind of logic, and it will be satisfied with the perception of one which is no more than tenuous, provided that it is sufficient to 'explain' a deep satisfaction experienced at other levels of the mind.[10] Where no logic can be perceived at the intellectual level, a dissatisfying confusion is felt. When audiences are asked why they have enjoyed the story of *Sir Gawain and the Green Knight*, they give the lord of the castle's explanations as to the reasons for the beheading game and the nature of his three blows as the source of their crowning satisfaction. They are delighted to hear that the magic of Morgan the Fay is the cause of it all and that Sir Gawain's virtue has been tested and appropriately rewarded and punished. The latter is an important logic which is comprehensible at the conscious level of our minds, but the former, while readily accepted as a reason, remains a mystery. We do not feel the urge to probe further into the nature of this witch and her magic. We are also given no explanation of the Green Chapel, and no audience asks for one. It is wholly satisfied with such explanations as are given.

Experience of story-telling leads one to the conclusion that, while our intellect demands some satisfaction and takes delight in fabliaux and trickster stories which achieve an ingenious logic at a conscious level, our most satisfying perception of logic in stories is that which is felt. By 'felt' is meant that spontaneous appreciation of appropriateness which takes place because we recognize that the content of the stories relates, in some way, to such basic human experiences as love, hate, fear and aspiration. The imparting of a story is an emotional affair. When we absorb it into our minds, recreating it there, we feel it. We can do this because it relates significantly to feelings which we have already experienced. We recognize its content because that content already exists in our own minds. The story is giving expression to feelings which we know. The reason why we cannot therefore explain the story fully is that our minds do not keep all that we know at a conscious level: that would be physically impossible and we also do not wish to be conscious of much that we know. Much of our knowledge and experience is therefore in the unconscious mind. The process of recognition takes place there, as well as at the conscious level. The emotional experience present in the story is recognized by our own emotional experience at a conscious and unconscious level and we then feel satisfaction. This satisfaction, even though it results from a comprehension which is far from wholly conscious, gives us all the pleasure we wish for from the story; boredom is our experience when we cannot recognize the story's content at any level in our minds.

These observations lead to the conclusion that *Sir Gawain and the Green Knight*—and *Little Red Riding-Hood*—have meaning; that is, that underlying the satisfactions we receive from the sound of the words with which they are told, and from those functions of the words which are appreciated by our intellect and our awareness of the outer world, there is deeper communication. In the Green Knight, the Green Chapel, the beheading, the experiences of the wilderness, the adventure in the second castle, and the dénouement we recognize emotional experiences which are profoundly important to us. How conscious this recognition is depends on the individual, but it is inevitable that a great deal of the recognition will be unconscious. The fact that a certain unconscious appreciation takes place is made clear only by the fact that our satisfaction in the stories is out of all proportion to their apparent content. Only those people who are more in touch with their unconscious than most have further foundations for conviction as to unconscious appreciation, and they too have a limited awareness. This will make the task of exploring meaning in a story a difficult one, but it will, in the course of this book, be made sufficiently to show that stories do have profound meaning for us.

Also to be observed from the experience of the told story is that it is a special time, deliberately created by the participants to be a time out of time, like a festival.[11] This is a very important factor where stories are concerned, but there is space here only to make a very few comments. The first is that in this time out of time which we create, we bring into being an artificial world in which we can temporarily live. This artificial world has both a coherence and a significance which is lacking in the ordinary course of life. In our created world, we have a temporary power to deal with things as we wish. One thing that we quite obviously do is isolate our emotional experiences: sorrow and joy, fear and reassurance, tend to be experienced separately, and, yet, their opposites will be present somewhere in the story. There is a forceful contrasting of feelings, this very contrast enabling us to experience each feeling powerfully; and as we isolate each feeling, we heighten and transfigure it. A striking example are the 'feast' and the 'nightmare' in *Sir Gawain and the Green Knight*.

The essence of the enjoyment which we obtain within our

6

specially created world is that we are suddenly made free to give full expression to the inner world of our minds, transforming it as we wish and thus transforming ourselves, bestowing upon our ordinariness a thrilling grandeur. This is how the story meets our needs and wishes, and we, in our turn, meet it by the process of identification. It is at this meeting-place, where the process of transmission finds recognition, that the meaning of story most profoundly lies. This meeting-place must now be sought in order to establish the observations made in this chapter and answer the many questions which must arise from them. The only means of seeking it is by making attempts to get in touch with one's unconscious, and the most obvious way in which one can do this is by studying dreams.

NOTES TO CHAPTER 1

1. See particularly: Laura Hibbard Loomis, *Adventures in the Middle Ages* (New York, 1962), pp. 295–9; R. S. Loomis, *Celtic Myth and Arthurian Romance* (New York, 1927); John Speirs, *Medieval English Poetry: The Non-Chaucerian Tradition* (London, 1957), pp. 215–51; 'Sir Gawain and the Green Knight', in *Scrutiny*, Vol. 16, No. 4 (1949); Jessie L. Weston, *From Ritual to Romance* (Cambridge, 1920).

2. Larry D. Benson, *Art and Tradition in Sir Gawain and the Green Knight* (New Brunswick, N.J., 1965), pp. 11–12.

3. See particularly: Albert B. Friedman, 'Morgan le Fay in Sir Gawain and the Green Knight', in *Sir Gawain and Pearl: Critical Essays*, edited by Robert J. Blanch (Indiana, 1966), pp. 152–3; Laura Hibbard Loomis, op. cit., pp. 293–308. J. R. Caldwell discusses the Fairy Mistress, Captive Maiden and Enchanted Princess motifs in the Introduction to his edition of *Eger and Grime*

(Harvard, 1933); MacEdward Leach discusses the motifs of the Two Brothers and the Faithful Servitor in the Introduction to his edition of *Amis and Amiloun*, E E T S 203 (1937).

4. John Speirs, 'Sir Gawain and the Green Knight', in *Scrutiny*, Vol. 16, No. 4 (1949), p. 289.

5. For studies relating to these oral origins, see particularly: Albert C. Baugh, 'Improvisation in the Middle English Romance', in the *Proceedings of the American Philosophical Society*, Vol. 103 (1959); Ruth Crosby, 'Oral Delivery in the Middle Ages', in *Speculum*, Vol. 11 (1936); Michael Curschmann, 'Oral Poetry in Medieval English, French and German Literature', in *Speculum*, Vol. 42 (1967); Ronald A. Waldron, 'Oral-Formulaic Technique and Middle English Alliterative Poetry', in *Speculum*, Vol. 32 (1957); Albert B. Lord, *The Singer of Tales* (Harvard and London, 1960).

6. The stories of *The King of the Golden Mountain*, *Cat-Skin*, *The Golden Bird* and *King Horn*, all discussed in succeeding chapters, provide examples which support this argument. These examples are referred to mainly, and only briefly, in the note sections. Unfortunately, a full investigation of this matter cannot be undertaken in this particular study.

7. These theories include the psycho-analytic theories of such writers as Jung and Marie-Louise von Franz. In their works, the comparative and symbolizing approaches are apparent, and the elements of stories tend to be studied out of context. Psycho-analytic studies, moreover, tend to use stories as sources of data, and they bring to the stories systems of psycho-analytic theory, complete with their mystifying jargon, which are treated as more important than the stories themselves. The stories are not studied on their own terms as works of literature.

8. Cosmo Pieterse, in a lecture on African Literature given for Voluntary Service Overseas in August 1971. He has edited several books on African literature and criticism, including *Seven South African Poets* (London, 1971).

9. Ruth Finnegan, *Oral Literature in Africa* (Oxford, 1970); *Limba Stories and Story-telling*, translated and edited by Ruth Finnegan (Oxford, 1967); Albert B. Lord, *The Singer of Tales* (Harvard and London, 1960); Antony Jones and June Buttrey, *Children and Stories* (Oxford, 1970).

10. Norman N. Holland, *The Dynamics of Literary Response* (New York, 1968), p. 185.

11. J. Huizinga, *Homo Ludens* (London, 1949); K. Kerényi, *The Religion of the Greeks and Romans* (London, 1962), Chapter 2, 'The Feast'.

2 Story as Dream

WHEN WE ARE asleep, we are more in touch with the feelings in our unconscious minds than we are when we are awake. We are alone with ourselves, no longer having to cope with the external world, and no longer influenced or interrupted by it.[1] Our intellect, with its powers of directed thinking,[2] a thinking which takes place with the use of words for the purpose of manipulating the external world and communicating with other people, is largely at rest. The moralizing aspect of our minds is also largely in suspense, but its continued, though less vigilant, activity is revealed in the evidence that the dream still feels the need to disguise, to some extent, those feelings to which it is giving expression. How is it giving expression to them? When dreaming, we do not think with our intellect, carefully finding words with which to express our thoughts; we think spontaneously and quite without effort, expressing these thoughts by means of pictures. This spontaneous thinking, with its language of images, will be called fantasy-thinking because it is essentially concerned with our feelings and has little interest in the reality-testing which is a prime concern of the intellect.

When we dream, we have feelings first and then we begin to think about them spontaneously and effortlessly, producing, as a result, a sequence of images. Thus our feelings, many of which are unconscious, become expressed in a certain language, the language which must be studied if an understanding is to be obtained of the activity in our unconscious minds, especially that of fantasy-thinking. The study of dreams is a study of a series of pictures, which may appear to be simple or weird, but which must never be assumed to be either. This pictorial language seeks both to express and disguise the contents of our minds. Thus, while dreams confront us with our inner world, much of which is unconscious in waking life, and give expression, with comparative freedom, to some of its content for our own private satisfaction, few of us know more about ourselves as a result, when we wake. We tend to look back upon the dream as nonsense, although it seemed to be totally real to us when we were asleep. However, we are aware of having felt satisfied, and this awareness is of profound significance. Satisfaction is only absent when the dream becomes a nightmare, and that occurs when the expression of our feelings frightens us.

9

The dream's only concern is our inner world; the outer world has become unconscious. Satisfaction and horror in dreams can therefore have nothing to do with outer realities separate from ourselves. An examination of dreams will help to show how far this is true also of the story, even though it is, in contrast to the dream, created in waking life (when there is an awareness of the realities of the outside world) and designed to be shared with others. Through an examination of dreams it is possible to show that they give meaningful expression to feelings, in the form of a kind of story created by the fantasy. In proving the existence of meaning at this level, and in showing that the sources of the dream are important, basic, feelings, it may be possible to throw light on the sources of the satisfaction which we experience in stories.

Great care was taken over the recording of the dreams which are to be studied,[3] and the dreamers themselves were equally concerned that their dreams should be meticulously recorded. They remembered the dreams clearly, and their later recalls corroborated the first recording. Indeed, while dreams may be looked upon as elusive experiences, impossible to record exactly, these dreams were recalled as if they had been actual waking experiences, and each event was of great importance to the dreamer.

The first of these dreams is that of a nine-year-old girl, Frances. She related it as follows:

I was on a rocky beach, the beach at Jenny Brown's Point, and my doll's house was there. The beach was very rocky and I wanted a spare room. I looked through the doll's house and just then Mummy and Gran appeared. Gran said 'Oh, what a beautiful little den'. Then I saw a den in front of me, with four rocks for desks and a bright yellow candlestick on each of them. Suddenly it was night and there were flames on the candles. I was in our garden, and Gran and Mummy had disappeared. I remembered it was Hallowe'en night and in front of me I saw a pretty little girl with yellow hair and blue eyes. I made friends with her. Then suddenly 11 o'clock struck and the girl became a witch and chased me with a wooden spoon. She still had golden hair under her black hat which puzzled me a bit. I felt she must really be a good witch. We chased each other round and round and then stilts appeared before me. Suddenly I was on them, running round and round the garden, feeling high and mighty.

Then I saw the golden-haired girl's mother and aunt. They were witches, dressed in black and with tall, black hats, like the witch who was chasing me. These witches were playing chess. I stole their White Queen and threw it at Mrs A, who was pas-

sing by. Mrs A shouted 'Pick up that litter!' 'In a moment!' I
snapped with an air of dignity, and I saw Mrs A's bathroom
light on. She was in the bath and I saw her with no clothes on.
I liked that. Then I quickly got the White Queen and threw it
at the golden-haired girl's mother and aunt.

Then I went into the house and there was a cauldron in the
middle of the sitting room. Kenneth and Martin [Frances'
brothers] were wizards stirring the cauldron. I was an ordinary girl. Kenneth and Martin were dressed in wizards' clothes
and looked rather lunatic. I felt a bit frightened about what
had happened to them and wondered what had happened to
Mummy and Gran. Then one o'clock struck, it was daylight
and everything vanished.

Frances related this dream with enjoyment, although it had
alarmed her a little too. When she described how she saw Mrs A in
the bathroom, she was self-conscious, but even that incident was
related with gusto. When asked if she was certain that she was an
'ordinary girl' at the end of the dream, she said 'yes', but in a way
which revealed that she had more insight into her dream than she
was willing to admit. Indeed, much of the feeling in the dream is
quite obvious to an outsider.

The second dream is that of a seven-year-old boy, Martin, and he
related it as follows:

We were going in the car with Daddy in the night, and
Daddy crashed into a wall. Then he went back to buy a new
car. I could hear birds flying about and thought at first that the
sound was a wolf. I and my friends walked through a tunnel
and in the distance we saw some hills which changed to some
very rocky, three-foot-high cliffs. We played around there and
I saw a boy with a dog and went up to talk to him. The dog
ran up to me and I realised that there wasn't a wolf but a dog
instead. A girl joined us.

Here Martin was confused, because he thought he knew who this
girl was: she seemed to him to be his sister, and yet he quickly
dismissed this association, because she seemed to be other people
too. He had no clear picture of her face. Then he continued:

The boy and girl ran away together and I couldn't run as
fast as them. Then I went over a steep hill and came to the
small rocky cliffs. My friends were there, and a ghost came
over the top of us. We all screamed, and ran under the rocks.
Then my friends started a game and I joined in. We stood half
a mile from the cliffs and when the sky turned very dark, we
had to run. The first one back to the cliffs waited to judge who

was the first back of all the others. The boy with the dog was standing on the cliff. I came first. The boys were scared of the haunted house nearby so they ran away over the top of a cliff; but I stopped halfway because I wasn't scared. The cliff shivered and fell, and the boys were killed. Then another lot of boys came, who looked just the same but didn't know me. They weren't scared, so we went back through the tunnel and ran towards the house. The dog ran behind and bumped into a tree in the path to the house and was killed. The girl peeped through a small little door and called us all to come because a man wanted our heads. The boys went into the house and I followed them in. I saw a pair of shoes and a pair of hands and a head. In his hands was an axe, and above the axe, on the wall, was written EM and two letters after that; I called the word EMIN. The man made us vanish and then he took us all and put us on two blocks with our necks over the gap between them. He chopped off our heads, and then he made us come back to life again without any heads. He put our heads back on us and stood us up. There was a line round our necks, but the axe had no blood on it. We walked down the corridor very slowly so that our heads wouldn't fall off. When we were quite far I remembered the magic word EMIN, so I said EMIN to make our heads come back to life again. Then our heads were fixed on again so that we could run back to the place where Daddy had a new car. And then we went home with Daddy.

Martin related this dream unselfconsciously, and, although he remembered it with some enjoyment, and was not disturbed enough by its final horror scene to be woken up, he called it a 'scary' dream. He showed no awareness at all of what it might mean. The series of events were recalled in great detail, and they aroused his keen interest. They were important events to him, but he was satisfied to understand them only at a superficial level. He never asked anyone why he dreamt the dream or what any of it meant. A month later, he talked of the dream once more, saying that he hoped he would never again have such a dream. He remembered the beheading scene as 'almost a nightmare', recalling what it felt like to be standing alive without a head.

There is space here only to examine certain characteristics of these dreams. Taking Frances' dream first, it is possible to trace a number of mental processes in it. The dreamer arranged the events in her dream in order to enjoy her feelings, and these feelings were, partly for this reason, split up, the dreamer first being 'very very good', and then being 'horrid'. When she was being 'very very good', the characters were recognizable, and when she was being 'horrid', two of them were unknown to her, while the third, Mrs A, was quite recognizable. The two unknown witches were the mother and aunt of the golden-haired girl, who was also unknown to the dreamer.

Why should Frances choose to be thinking about all these unknown people? Surely it is far more likely that she was thinking about people whom she knew, as she was where she herself and her relatives and passer-by were concerned. Let us assume that her dream has a logic and that a recognition of the pattern of split feelings will help to find it. When Frances was celebrating feelings of which she could wholly approve, she did not employ disguise, but when she wished to celebrate feelings which she deemed to be 'wicked', she felt the need to disguise their exact nature. She allowed herself to be aware that she was the perpetrator of the 'wicked' acts, because she wanted the enjoyment of this awareness, but she did not allow herself to know who the 'witches' were. It must be significant that she did not know who they were while she did know who Mrs A was.

In the first scene, we have the dreamer and two relatives, while in the defiant scene we have the dreamer, the two relatives of someone else, and Mrs A. The first two relatives are recognizable and approving; the second two are unknown and witches. Mrs A is distinct in not being a relative. If one assumes that the 'good' scene and the 'bad' one are parallel scenes, the dream might be seen to be highly logical, and this fact can, as far as possible where a dream is concerned, be established. The dreamer would hardly be concerning herself with people unknown to her, and it is known that her first thoughts were about herself, her mother and her grandmother in a loving situation. Her next thoughts, it may be presumed, were about the same people in a hating situation. The dreamer expressed her change of feeling visually, seeing herself as a good, golden-haired girl who then changed into a witch, which is how she saw herself when she wished to be 'wicked'. She nevertheless retained a revealing awareness of the golden-haired goodness combined with the blackness of a witch under the same black hat. She then turned her mother and grandmother into witches whom she would defy; she proclaimed them to be wholly wicked black witches who deserved to have their White Queen thrown at them, while she herself was not a witch.

Frances did not recognize the golden-haired girl who became a witch, as a picture of herself, and she therefore did not recognize the golden-haired girl's relatives as her own. She was going through a process of denial, an essential part of her system of disguises. She did not feel the necessity of denial when she threw the White Queen at Mrs A and then stripped her naked, because she did not love

13

Mrs A as she loved her relatives. There was not the same conflict of mixed feelings where Mrs A was concerned, the love feelings making the dreamer wish to deny those of hate. Frances did not transform Mrs A into a 'secret, black and midnight hag' either: this woman did not have to be wholly wicked in order to be attacked without feelings of guilt. The dreamer's feelings about her were not strong enough to bring about such extremes as this.

While a logic has been emerging in the dream, several interesting features have consequently become apparent. Still more can be discerned. Above all, it can be seen that there were not nearly so many characters in this dream as there seemed to be. Three of them were Frances herself, and five of them were all playing identical rôles: the rôle of the female, adult 'authority figure' of the maternal type. The brothers were wizards at the end, in contrast to the 'fact' that the dreamer was an 'ordinary girl' and not a witch.

As she wove her dream, Frances fragmented personality by the process of splitting. It is easier to contemplate personality if we split up its complexity into bits, creating many people who are really all bits of one person. We not only find it simpler, but also more comforting, for we can feel confused and frightened by the reality of the complexity of personality, with all its ambivalence of feeling and elusiveness of mood. Splitting is also fun. Frances enjoyed being all-good and then all-bad, and the colourful figures which we can conjure up to express these split-up emotional experiences, like the angel and the witch, are entertaining. They also give interest and splendour to our feelings, which Frances' 'ordinariness' at the end of the dream hardly does. Indeed, she had no desire for this ordinariness at all, and really saw herself as a witch at that moment.

Turning to Martin's dream, there is again space only for the study of certain features—those which can be most readily discerned and are most helpful to this investigation. This dream seems a jumble of events, and yet it can be seen that they take place within the framework of being with 'Daddy' in his car. At the beginning and end of the dream, Martin was thinking about his father in contrasting ways. Within this framework are five distinguishable scenes. In the first, Martin met a boy and a girl who left him out of their relationship: they ran away together and he could not keep up with them. In the second scene, came the ghost, which expressed both Martin's thrill and his fear. In the third, Martin ran fastest up to the boy, when 'the sky turned very dark'. Then follows a scene of terror and death. The fifth scene is that of the beheading, the very detail of which conveys its importance to the dreamer.

The most effective way of studying the characters, most of whom are nameless, is by looking at their rôles. The rôle of Martin's companions is indistinguishable from that of Martin in some respects (they were even beheaded under the same blow), but wholly distinct in other, significant respects: they, for instance, lost the race while Martin won it. The two groups of companions were equally identical with each other, and yet wholly distinct, in their rôles in the dream. Of the other characters, there was one female, whom Martin associated a little with his sister. She appeared to be seen as a kind of ally to male characters, in a sense *vis-à-vis* Martin—first in the case of the boy with the dog, and then in the case of the beheading man. Her rôles also give an impression that the boy with the dog and the beheading man were linked in their rôles. Beyond this, one can only speculate, and it has already been possible to discern enough to observe some interesting factors about the nature of the characters in the dream.

The magic word is another feature of the dream which can be fruitfully studied. Martin himself was, of course, creating the events of the dream: they were brought about by his wishes. However, it can be seen that there are many, and opposing, feelings in the dream, and that Martin both wished and did not wish for some of the experiences in it. Some of his wishes terrified him. Without having to speculate as to the exact nature of his feelings and wishes, it can be seen that Martin felt the need to gain control over those that opposed the ones which he desired ultimately to triumph. The 'magic word' was a formula which gave him a sense of controlling power.

Is it possible to discern any leads in the dream which would help one to discover a coherent theme? The fact that it begins and ends with Martin's father suggests that Martin was thinking of his father a great deal. There also appears to be a change of feeling about him: at the beginning Martin had him do something stupid, and at the end he restored him. In the beheading scene, Martin proved himself able to reverse the beheading power of the axe-man, and the terror was over. It was then that he conjured up his father again in a new light. What evidence is there for the meaning of the beheading incident? All that can definitely be said is that subsequent events show that the incident was not about death: it appears to be an image expressing something else.

There is really no need to follow up these leads with speculation, in this particular discussion. Enough has been observed to show that, crazy as the dream may appear at first sight, it does, in fact, have a certain kind of coherent thinking at its centre, and a decided form.

The studies of the dreams also reveal that their pictorial language is a dynamic and personal language, chosen by the dreamer to express his particular feelings at the moment of dreaming. It is important to note the complexity of the images. Frances' White

15

Queen, for instance, is female, royal, powerful in the game of chess, adult and white. While Frances was feeling defiant and 'wicked', she picked up such a figure and threw it at female, powerful and adult characters, whose authority might be pictured as royal and whose insistence upon 'goodness' rather than 'badness' might be pictured as white. They were the owners of the White Queen, and Frances made them black 'queens', throwing their white one at them.

Another important point that has arisen in this study is that while the dreamers made things happen as they wished, many features of the drama, in each case, arose from the fact that conflicting wishes were at work.

It would be interesting now to see what is happening when a person in the waking state embarks on the creation of a story. Let us return to the dreamer, Frances, to see how she has created stories.

At the age of five years, she wrote the following story:

> Once upon a time there was a little queen and she went for a walk in the woods.

The following year she wrote this story:

> There was once a poor girl called Kay. She was only about six when her mother and father died. Kay had no friends or relashons to look after her so she had to look after herself. She had no treasures only a red cape to keep her warm. Her house had fallen down so she had no house to live in, so she just sat with her cape on. She was a pritty little girl and everybody loved her. One day Queen Mary heard about her and called her there.

At the age of seven, Frances wrote 'How Gillian came to live with the Princess', and the story went as follows:

> Gillian stood in the garden very sad. She did not like home at all, she did not like Mummy and Daddy.
>
> Oh dear she said what shall I do? I know, I shall go away from Mum and Dad and camp with a tent.
>
> Soon she came to a lovely house and gave a nock on the door and there stood a lovely princess. Soon they made friends and Gillian told the princess why she came. Then the princess said will you live with me? Yes I will said Gillian. So they had grate fun and nice games.
>
> One day Gillian said to the princess will you call me your sister? Yes said the princess I will and I will make you a princess. So they grew very happy and lived happily ever after. The end.

16

The most striking difference between these stories and the dreams is that they are not about the creator of them: they are about 'Kay' and 'Gillian'. However, experiences which are not recognized as existing in our own minds are felt to be boring, and the effort of writing a story would only be expended on emotional experience of profound importance to the story-teller. Frances and Kay were the same age, but it is clear, without this information, that Frances was identified with Kay and Gillian: she herself was both of them. Just as she was the protagonist in her dream, so she was the protagonist in her stories. In her dream, she was aware in part that the protagonist was herself, while being unaware that the golden-haired girl was also herself. In the private story of her dream she was happy to be aware of her involvement in the story, and only felt the need to hide some aspects of her involvement from herself.

In her stories she pretended that she was not involved at all. She created them because she wished to share a day-dream with an audience, and it was essential for her free enjoyment in this sharing that no one should know the identity of the heroine, perhaps not even herself. In creating her stories, she would have been hoping that other people would join her in her enjoyment of them. They would do this by recognizing the day-dreams as within their own experience and feeling free to become the heroine in each one without there being any need for anyone to know that this was what was taking place. It is important to note at this point that 'Kay' and 'Gillian' were not the names of anyone in Frances' circle at the time of the creation of the stories.

Frances created her stories to express her personal feelings, and yet a resemblance to traditional stories can be discerned. The heroines leave home, pass through a brief situation in a wilderness and finally attain royal splendour in some way. In the first story, the heroine is royal from the outset—another familiar feature of traditional story. However, at this stage of this investigation, it could hardly be claimed that Frances was merely imitating familiar stories—and not only because her stories have their own distinct inspiration and characteristics. Even where Frances may be influenced by traditional stories, this speaks for the great importance of their content: no traditional story could be of interest to her unless it spoke tellingly to her own emotional experience. Shared stories, whether newly created or traditional, appear to have the same source: our shared inner experience.

It might, at this stage, be reasonable to suppose that Frances, in becoming a story-teller, was engaging in an activity no different from that of the story-tellers before her who created and recreated our traditional literature. They wished to share a day-dream, and

17

found a response in others, who recognized it as giving particularly satisfying form to emotional experience of their own.

These shared day-dreams have a similarity to nocturnal dreams, but there are notable differences. Their imagery and structure are strikingly more coherent and intelligible to the conscious mind than are those of dreams, and the protagonist is always in disguise: he is a displacement for those who enjoy the story.

In Frances' three stories can be traced a development from the purely dreamlike and magical to similarly dreamlike and magical material which has been made slightly more rational and coherent, for the greater satisfaction of an audience aware of the realities of the outer world. In shared stories, the intellect's powers are employed to organize the spontaneous products of fantasy into a form more pleasing and intelligible to the conscious mind. Nevertheless, it appears from the study of Frances' stories that, like dreams, stories are fundamentally the expression of feelings, which are transformed by fantasy-thinking into a sequence of images. This pictorial sequence is conveyed to others by means of words, which do not diverge from the images, although the intellectual thinking from which they spring uses them to give the story greater coherence and to provide rationalizations. Thus our powers of directed thinking do not usually give stories, in their entirety, the kind of logic with which we are concerned in everyday life. Most stories only make complete sense at the level of fantasy, as do dreams.

Therefore, the study of dreams must throw light on the sources of satisfaction which we experience when contemplating stories. However, this cannot be appreciated without a deeper understanding of the activity of fantasy. It is now time to study this activity: the defences, the imagery, and the sequences of events created, as fantasy gives shape to feeling.[4] This will be done through detailed study of stories.

NOTES TO CHAPTER 2

1. Erich Fromm, *The Forgotten Language* (London, 1952), Chapter on 'The Nature of Dreams'.

2. C. G. Jung, *Symbols of Transformation* (London, 1952), pp. 13, 16–20.

3. It was imperative for the study to obtain authentic 'texts' of the dreams. They were first recounted informally in September 1973, and were then immediately retold by the dreamers for the recorder, who recorded the dreams verbatim without comment. The dreamers were then asked to clarify their images: for example, what did Frances's witches look like? Later in the day, the dreamers were asked to retell their dreams while the recorder checked the first records. The records were not read back to the dreamers. These second accounts tallied with the first ones, except that Frances had recalled a further detail of her dream, the fact that she had walked on stilts. The dreamers were asked to give every detail they could remember: so often, details which are important are discounted by dreamers as unimportant. The dreams remained vivid in the dreamers' minds a month later, and nearly two years later.

As Martin grew more articulate, he communicated more of his dream, and he also drew pictures of it which included detail which he had not put into words (for example, the birds and the execution block). In his first account of the beheading scene, Martin only gave us a bare outline of the events; later we were given a fuller description, and it was quite clear that this contained no more than genuine memories of the dream.

Great care was taken to prevent distortion of the 'texts' of the dreams by ideas and interpretations of the recorder or anyone else. This was not difficult, since the dreamers were too deeply concerned with their dreams to allow any alteration to take place. They wished their dreams to be meticulously recorded.

No definite explanation of 'Emin' can be argued; but it is possible that Martin was thinking of his own name, the first letter of 'Martin' being 'M' and his second forename being 'Emmet'.

4. It might well be argued at this stage that this study should be using the term 'imagination', not 'fantasy'. I have chosen the term 'fantasy' in order to emphasize that the mental activity involved is one concerned with the preoccupations of the inner world, with preoccupations which are fundamentally separate from and unmodified by the intellect's concerns, and the exterior world. 'Imagination' encompasses the meaning of 'fantasy', but it also encompasses other creative activities of the mind which are more directed and which may also show concern with the outer world. While these powers are undoubtedly also involved in the creation of stories, it seems important not to complicate further a discussion already complicated enough, and to use the term which directs attention firmly towards the particular characteristics of the mental activity under scrutiny.

3 Story and Fantasy

IT HAS BEEN seen that as the dreamer is the protagonist of his dream, so is the creator of a story the protagonist of his story. That the listener to a story is similarly identified with the protagonist of the story must be the key to his involvement: he enters the story as the protagonist, and he does so in disguise. There he experiences the adventures as if they were his own. At the conscious and intellectual level of his mind, he may not be at all aware of this, but, where his feelings are concerned, the need to identify and experience is urgent. Feelings are given expression, within the special world of the story, by the spontaneous, imaginative thinking which we call fantasy. As we listen to the story, we too are thinking on the level of fantasy and, unconsciously at least, understand its language. Recognition takes place, as the individual fantasy meets the fantasy of the story, and grasps its logic.

Let us see what happens if a detailed study is made of a traditional story, bringing all that has so far been observed to the task. The traditional story to be studied will be a folktale from the collection made by the Brothers Grimm.[1]

THE KING OF THE GOLDEN MOUNTAIN

A certain merchant had two children, a son and daughter, both very young and scarcely able to run alone. He had two richly laden ships then making a voyage upon the seas, in which he had embarked all his property, in the hope of making great gains, when the news came that they were lost. Thus from being a rich man he became very poor, so that nothing was left him but one small plot of land; and, to relieve his mind a little of his trouble, he often went out to walk there.

One day, as he was roving along, a little rough-looking dwarf stood before him, and asked him why he was so sorrowful, and what it was that he took so deeply to heart. But the merchant replied, 'If you could do me any good, I would tell you.' 'Who knows but I may,' said the little man. 'Tell me what is the matter, and perhaps I can be of some service.' Then the merchant told him how all his wealth was gone to the bottom of the sea, and how he had nothing left except that little plot of

20

land. 'Oh, trouble not yourself about that,' said the dwarf; 'only promise to bring me here, twelve years hence, whatever meets you first on your return home, and I will give you as much gold as you please.' The merchant thought this was no great request; that it would most likely be his dog, or something of that sort, but forgot his little child: so he agreed to the bargain, and signed and sealed the engagement to do what was required.

But as he drew near home, his little boy was so pleased to see him, that he crept behind him and laid fast hold of his legs. Then the father started with fear, and saw what it was that he had bound himself to do; but as no gold was come, he consoled himself by thinking that it was only a joke that the dwarf was playing him.

About a month afterwards he went upstairs into an old lumber room to look for some old iron, that he might sell it and raise a little money; and there he saw a large pile of gold lying on the floor. At the sight of this he was greatly delighted, went into trade again, and became a greater merchant than before.

Meantime his son grew up, and as the end of the twelve years drew near, the merchant became very anxious and thoughtful; so that care and sorrow were written upon his face. The son one day asked what was the matter: but his father refused to tell for some time; at last, however, he said that he had, without knowing it, sold him to a little ugly-looking dwarf for a great quantity of gold; and that the twelve years were coming round when he must perform his agreement. Then the son said, 'Father, give yourself very little trouble about that; depend upon it, I shall be too much for the little man.'

When the time came, they went out together to the appointed place; and the son drew a circle on the ground, and set himself and his father in the middle. The little dwarf soon came, and said to the merchant, 'Have you brought me what you promised?' The old man was silent, but his son answered, 'What do you want here?' The dwarf said, 'I come to talk with your father, not with you.' 'You have deceived and betrayed my father,' said the son; 'give him up his bond.' 'No,' replied the other, 'I will not yield up my rights.' Upon this a long dispute arose; and at last it was agreed that the son should be put into an open boat, that lay on the side of a piece of water hard by, and that the father should push him off with his own hand; so that he should be turned adrift. Then he took leave of his father, and set himself in the boat; and as it was pushed off it heaved, and fell on one side into the water: so the merchant thought that his son was lost, and went home very sorrowful.

But the boat went safely on, and did not sink; and the young

21

man sat securely within, till at length it ran ashore upon an unknown land. As he jumped upon the shore, he saw before him a beautiful castle, but empty and desolate within, for it was enchanted. At last, however, he found a white snake in one of the chambers.

Now the white snake was an enchanted Princess; and she rejoiced greatly to see him, and said, 'Art thou at last come to be my deliverer? Twelve long years have I waited for thee, for thou alone canst save me. This night twelve men will come: their faces will be black, and they will be hung round with chains. They will ask what thou dost here; but be silent, give no answer, and let them do what they will—beat and torment thee. Suffer all, only speak not a word, and at twelve o'clock they must depart. The second night twelve others will come; and the third night twenty-four, who will even cut off thy head; but at the twelfth hour of that night their power is gone, and I shall be free, and will come and bring thee the water of life, and will wash thee with it, and restore thee to life and health.' And all came to pass as she had said; the merchant's son spoke not a word, and the third night the Princess appeared, and fell on his neck and kissed him; joy and gladness burst forth throughout the castle; the wedding was celebrated, and he was King of the Golden Mountain.

They lived together very happily, and the Queen had a son. Eight years had passed over their heads when the King thought of his father: and his heart was moved, and he longed to see him once again. But the Queen opposed his going, and said, 'I know well that misfortunes will come.' However, he gave her no rest till she consented. At his departure she presented him with a wishing-ring, and said, 'Take this ring, and put it on your finger; whatever you wish it will bring you: only promise that you will not make use of it to bring me hence to your father's.' Then he promised what she asked, and put the ring on his finger, and wished himself near the town where his father lived. He found himself at the gates in a moment; but the guards would not let him enter, because he was so strangely clad. So he went up to a neighbouring mountain where a shepherd dwelt, and borrowed his old frock, and thus passed unobserved into the town. When he came to his father's house, he said he was his son; but the merchant would not believe him, and said he had had but one son, who he knew was long since dead: and as he was only dressed like a poor shepherd, he would not even offer him anything to eat. The King, however, persisted that he was his son, and said, 'Is there no mark by which you would know if I am really your son?' 'Yes,' observed his mother, 'our son has a mark like a raspberry under the right arm.' Then he showed them the mark, and they were satisfied that what he had said was true. He next told them how he was King of the Golden Mountain, and was married to a Princess, and had a son seven years old. But the merchant said, 'That can never be true; he must be a fine king truly who travels about in a shepherd's frock.' At this the son was very angry; and, forgetting his promise, turned his ring, and wished for his Queen and son. In an instant they stood before him; but the Queen wept, and said he had broken his word, and misfortune would follow. He did all he could to soothe her, and she at last appeared to be appeased; but she was not so in reality, and only meditated how she should take her revenge.

One day he took her to walk with him out of the town, and showed her the spot where the boat was turned adrift upon the wide waters. Then he sat himself down, and said, 'I am very much tired; sit by me, I will rest my head in your lap, and sleep a while.' As soon as he had fallen asleep, however, she drew the ring from his finger, and crept softly away, and wished herself and her son at home in their kingdom. And when the King awoke, he found himself alone, and saw that the ring was gone from his finger. 'I can never return to my father's house,' said he; 'they would say I am a sorcerer: I will journey forth into the world till I come again to my kingdom.'

So saying, he set out and travelled till he came to a mountain, where three giants were sharing their inheritance; and as they saw him pass, they cried out and said, 'Little men have sharp wits; he shall divide the inheritance between us.' Now it consisted of a sword that cut off an enemy's head whenever the wearer gave the words 'Heads off!'; a cloak that made the owner invisible, or gave him any form he pleased; and a pair of boots that transported the person who put them on wherever he wished. The King said they must first let him try these wonderful things, that he might know how to set a value upon them. Then they gave him the cloak, and he wished himself a fly, and in a moment he was a fly. 'The cloak is very well,' said he; 'now give me the sword.' 'No,' said they, 'not unless you promise not to say "Heads off!" for if you do, we are all dead men.' So they gave it him on condition that he tried its virtue only on a tree. He next asked for the boots also; and the moment he had all three in his possession he wished himself at the Golden Mountain; and there he was in an instant. So the giants were left behind with no inheritance to divide or quarrel about.

As he came near to the castle he heard the sound of merry music; and the people around told him that his Queen was about to celebrate her marriage with another Prince. Then he threw his cloak around him, and passed through the castle, and placed himself by the side of his Queen, where no one saw him. But when anything to eat was put upon her plate, he took it away and ate it himself; and when a glass of wine was handed to her, he took and drank it: and thus, though they kept on serving her with meat and drink, her plate continued always empty.

Upon this, fear and remorse came over her, and she went into her chamber and wept; and he followed her there. 'Alas!' said she to herself, 'did not my deliverer come? Why then doth enchantment still surround me?'

'Thou traitress,' said he, 'thy deliverer indeed came, and now is near thee: has he deserved this of thee?' And he went out and dismissed the company, and said the wedding was at an end, for that he was returned to his kingdom: but the princes and nobles and counsellors mocked at him. However, he would enter into no parley with them, but only demanded whether they would depart in peace, or not. Then they turned and tried to seize him; but he drew his sword, and, with a word, the traitors' heads fell before him; and he was once more King of the Golden Mountain.

What is the point of such a story as this? In many ways it appears ridiculous. The sophisticated listener who is not content simply to enjoy it, might be tempted to compare it with novels and wonder why we do not find any attempt to present the characters as whole personalities, living in a social setting which is realistically described. Within a brief span, the narrative rushes us through a large number of events, all portrayed by vivid, and often lurid, images, many violent and all extraordinary. It is impossible to decide which event is the most inexplicable: the merchant's crazy promise to the sinister dwarf, the decision to expose the youth, the Queen's injunction that she and the hero's father must not meet, or the giants' foolishness. All is mystification. The familiarity of most of the events as typical events in story does not help us to explain them. Many a father unwittingly promises his child to a sinister character, in story, and many a character is set adrift in a boat, and yet these events still make no more sense to our reasoning faculties than do the crude activities in the later part of the story, when all is magic and the story's outcome depends upon whose magic prevails. But any accusations of this nature against the story can be seen to be as ridiculous as the story itself appears to be. Those who laugh at the story will just as quickly discount the accusations as inappropriate. The story, it will be claimed, is not concerned with the reality of everyday affairs.

What is it concerned with then? It is clearly concerned with something. This old story has long given and still gives a satisfaction which suggests that an inner logic is recognized, resulting in the story's being appreciated and transmitted from generation to generation. Moreover, the story can be seen to have a highly formalized structure, which could hardly have come into being unless it is purposefully giving form to a decided logic.

Standing back from the story for a moment, and contemplating this form, a repetition can be discerned. The youth leaves his home on a journey and arrives at a castle where there is a mysterious woman. He marries her, after triumphing in a fearsome adventure lasting three nights, and, as she is a 'princess' and he is her 'deliverer', he becomes a king. Then he returns home, arrives in disguise and achieves the recognition of his parents that he is a king, at the cost of being abandoned by his queen at the very same place where he had been abandoned by his father and the dwarf. He therefore sets off on another journey from home, this time specifically in search of his kingdom, and he has another adventure, which this time involves three giants and three magical objects. His triumph in this adventure brings about a reaffirmation of his marriage and royalty.

Let us now leave this position outside the story and take up a new position inside it. It may be possible to discover the logic of this story by looking for it from a position in the mind of the youth, contemplating the story as his creation in the language of fantasy. Accordingly, one may start as follows: This is the youth's story and he arranges it all. He gives himself a rich father who has become poor, a sister, and a mother whom he does not mention until he visualizes himself at home again half-way through his story. By means of the incident with the dwarf, the hero arranges that he should leave home, and this is the beginning of his adventure. He deliberately sends himself into exile so that he might transfer himself to a place of adventure. All this seems somewhat unlikely and it raises many new questions, but a definite link between the initial situation and that in the place of adventure is clinched by the twelve years during which both the dwarf and the princess wait for the youth: this indicates that he has been making careful, unacknowledged plans.

At first it seems as though the merchant is the hero, but the youth soon takes his place. The mother and sister receive scant attention, the sister alone being mentioned in the first scene at home, and the mother alone in the second. These factors are all strange and make the most sense if one approaches them as thoughts in the youth's mind. He is thinking about his feelings, and seeking both to express them and disguise them. The fact that the sister and the mother stand in for each other, as it were, must be significant. Each time the hero thinks of his home it contains a father and a female relative, and there appears to be a deliberate ambiguity and studied casualness about the way he treats the latter throughout his story.

If one pursues the theory that these relatives are figments of the youth's mind, the rest of the characters will also be figments of his mind. They will be images which only have significance in relation to his feelings. First we have the dwarf, then the princess, and then the blackened men in chains, the three giants, the rival prince and the courtiers.

What feelings does the dwarf represent? It is his trick, deceiving the father, which brings about the exile of the hero. He is a little shrivelled trickster who obtains the hero for gold and who is too much for the father and son together, both grown men. As a result of his game, the hero arrives at the beautiful, empty castle, containing the white snake which is an enchanted princess. When one moves inside the story, one can see its repetitive nature much more clearly than one can from a position outside it. One can see that there is a repetition of the idea of a little trickster outwitting those greater in size, this idea being, first, an important initial one, when the dwarf tricks the father, and then recurring towards the end of the story, when the little trickster is the hero himself and those outwitted are giants. In each case, the trickster's aim is theft, first of all surreptitious theft, buying off the victim in order to obtain something of greater value, and then overt theft. Both sequences of images throw light on each other, and it can be seen that they express the same feelings, those feelings being, it is apparent, those of the same person, the hero. The dwarf must be the hero himself, and its ugly, shrunken appearance must express how he feels about himself as he tricks his father.

What trick is the hero really playing on his father? It must be one which he sees as wicked, because he both expresses it and disguises it as the machinations of an ugly dwarf. He represents himself as separate from the dwarf and as having nothing to do with him; he appears as the dwarf's victim. Under cover of this elaborate disguise, the hero gives his father the slip in his mind. That which he next visualizes must help to reveal why he does this: it must give a more complete picture of the hero's feelings. It is in fact a castle, empty of people, full of magic, and containing a white snake which is the way in which the hero sees the princess who has been waiting for him to rescue her for twelve years. The rescue will involve torment and beheading for three nights running at the hands of blackened, chained men. The adventure ends in triumph, the hero gaining the princess, who heals him, and also the mysterious kingdom of the 'Golden Mountain'.

This sequence of images is only briefly described, expressing

26

rapid thoughts upon which the hero does not dwell. He first sees a castle, surrounded by water, and then a white snake in one of its chambers. This snake is the same as a princess in his mind. He thinks of them both, first the snake and then the princess, and they are one in his mind. The former is the latter but he must make it look like the latter, with no trace of the former remaining, by enduring the torments and beheading of the chained men. The faces of these men are blackened, but the snake is seen as white. These images, when examined carefully, reveal more about the feelings which, apparently, have been in the hero's mind from the beginning. The lady is royal and surrounded by magic; she is associated with a white snake. The hero can only reach her surreptitiously, and gaining her is associated first with his own miserable trickery and then with his endurance of torment and beheading. All these events are arranged by the hero, impelled by his wishes, but they will not be wholly a controlled arrangement on his part: compulsive feelings will have played a part in summoning them up. They follow inevitably upon the hero's indulgence of certain feelings, the initial feelings, and attendant wishes, which give rise to the story. They spring from the many and conflicting feelings which the hero experiences where the initial feelings are concerned; and, it must also be remembered, however much the imagery may appear to represent the feelings of other people, imagery must always relate, essentially, to the hero's feelings about himself.

Every detail of these images needs close attention, for all are significant. They will not be discussed in detail here, since the prime purpose of this discussion is to explore the approach and methods of thinking which help to reveal the entire story as making coherent sense.

The lady seems to be a particularly significant image, and she is invested with all the hero's wishes, while he denies them. In our first picture of her, she is in the grip of an unidentified power which is, in fact, the hero's power, although the power is governed by the way in which he sees her. While the imagery and events associated with her express the hero's vision of her as taboo for particular reasons, he also arranges that she is in collusion with him. However, the wishes which achieve this are counteracted by opposite wishes: to use the very words which he speaks to the dwarf, he feels that he has 'deceived and betrayed' his father, and this fills him with anger against his dwarf self. At the same time, he refuses, in his words as the dwarf, to 'yield up' his 'rights'.

Immediately upon meeting the loving snake, the hero sees an overpowering number of frightening male figures, with blackened faces and in chains, making a threatening approach to ask him what he is doing in the lady's castle. His heroic endurance of their

27

torments and beheading dispels the magic which has surrounded the princess and produced the chained men, and this leaves him able to see the princess as a woman whom he may marry, this marriage, in its turn, making him 'King of the Golden Mountain'. The magic has been, in part, the hero's sense of the power of his own self-threatening feelings; in his triumph over them he is left only with the magic which wishes him well. According to the logic of everyday affairs, there is no reason why the hero should now be a king; from whom is he inheriting his kingdom? One might also ask exactly what this kingdom is. The answer must lie in an imaginative comprehension of the image 'Golden Mountain', and here one must bear in mind its many attributes, particularly its golden quality, its soaring shape, and its connection with the lady and all the hero's feelings about her.

The chained men can be seen to have multiple significance, while they chiefly represent that aspect of the hero which is in agreement that he should receive appropriate punishment for the thoughts which he has been entertaining. The hero, however, enjoys his exciting and heroic experience, especially as he has given himself a magic which will protect him. He puts into the princess's mouth a description of the ordeal, in which it is specifically stated to last only for a given time, after which he will be restored to his princess.

The chained men are numbered in a ritual fashion, as also is time in this story. These numbers relate to each other and help one to see how the images in the story are linked. There will also be other factors behind the hero's numbering the chained men as he does. Further details, such as the chains and the blackened faces, will be complex in their significance: the blackened faces will, over and above their associations with evil and dirt, be a disguise.

As one moves into the remaining part of the story, one is constantly aware of repetition. It is now everywhere apparent. The next adventure begins when the hero has clearly taken the place which his father had in the initial situation. He is the father of a son of about the same age as he is at the beginning of his story, and his queen emerges as dominant and the possessor of formidable magical powers. She is a maternal figure, as seen through the eyes of a child, and it is no longer a surprise that misfortune will result if she is visualized together with the hero's father. However, the hero wishes to declare his triumph to his father.

Arming himself with his queen's ring on his finger, he thinks of himself approaching his father. He has, in fact, armed himself with a powerful sense of his sexual union with his queen, as the queen 'put the ring on his finger', but, as he approaches his father, he feels that he cannot do so as a king. He would only be acceptable as a shepherd. When he visualizes the meeting, his mother is there too, and both his parents go through a rite of recognizing him as their son by means of a recognition mark. Next he wishes them to recognize him as 'King of the Golden Mountain', married to a princess and father of a son aged seven, but his parents refuse to believe that this shepherd son is really a king. The hero feels a shepherd before his parents and, in anger and desperation, he confronts his parents with his queen and son. The result is a sense of the loss of his queen's love. Returning in his mind to the place where he had first set out to meet her, he visualizes her withdrawing her ring from his finger and vanishing with their son.

As soon as he conjures up a scene where he, as a king, with a queen and son, confronts his parents, sorrow and anger are expressed. It is the queen who expresses these feelings, no feelings being openly assigned to the parents. Then the hero loses all sense of possession of the queen and the son, and sets out to regain this sense from the very place where he last set out. This time he is open about his desire for the kingdom, while his first setting-out is represented as brought about by others. This second departure echoes the true nature of the first. As he leaves, he thinks of himself as a sorcerer and, indeed, his determination to be so has increased. He turns his back on his home where he feels a powerless little boy vis-à-vis his parents.

Instead, he makes another attempt to overcome this feeling that he is a powerless little boy. In the scene with the giants, which echoes other incidents of the story in a variety of significant ways, there are two important new factors. The trickster hero leaves himself undisguised and unchanged in size: the disguises have been reversed, and the emphasis is on the vast size of the magical fathers rather than on the small, shrunken appearance of the hero.

Having made the giants' powers separate from them and portable, so that he can acquire them, the hero summons up a vision of his queen being married to another prince, and vanquishes it with these powers. Thus he overcomes all opposing feelings, and achieves victory for his paramount wishes. His story comes to a natural end.

In this rather infantile story, there is no attempt to satisfy the mature mind as to how the hero can achieve a solution to his conflicts. Here, childish delight in the power of omnipotent wishes is paramount, and all problems can be solved by obtaining the magical powers of father-figures. He sees these powers as embodied in objects so that they can be stolen, but also so that they will be tangible and fixed when in his own possession, unlike his magic wishes, which are fleeting through his mind one after another, impossible to capture and hold, and constantly causing conflict as they oppose each other. Such magic as this is less powerful than the magic of the fathers, and only when he obtains the magic of the fathers can the hero be powerful like a father. He can then take the place of the giant magicians by the mountain as 'King of the Golden Mountain'. Being this 'king' is presented as being a matter of being married to the 'queen', but, striking among the many attributes of the 'Golden Mountain' are those expressing the hero's soaring ambition and desire to be gigantic and splendid. At the end of his story it seems that such thoughts are at the forefront of his mind; there is no return of tender love. The queen remains his queen, as her remarriage is cancelled out, and therefore he is a 'king', possessor of the 'queen', and, above all, of total power.

It appears, from this brief analysis, as if a logic in the story has been discovered, a logic which is experienced at the level of our feelings. It also appears that all the elements of a story are seen from the correct point of view if one takes up a position in the mind of the hero, seeing the story as his creation. The meaning discovered in the story, as a result of this brief identification with the hero, is by no means all the meaning that may be discerned in it, but the purpose here is not to discover all that the story means, but whether meaning, in a logical and important sense, can be found at all in this tale, and, if so, how.

The key to the logic of traditional story appears to be a matter of taking the long-recognized phenomenon of identification with the hero to its logical conclusion. All those who enjoy a story join the story-teller as the protagonist of his story: the story-teller, the audience and the protagonist are therefore united in the process of creating and recreating the story. Everything that takes place should be viewed as having been arranged by the protagonist: the characters and events are figments of his mind. Technically, 'the protagonist' (or the 'hero' or 'heroine') is the character whom we acknowledge to be playing this rôle. He is how we most wish to see ourselves in the story, and while he is as much an image as are other characters representing the hero in the story, it is correct to see him as the essential representative of ourselves, creating the story. We, if we join the story-teller, are the actual hero, recreating the story through the acknowledged hero.

Viewing the events of a story as the creation of the protagonist, is the beginning, rather than the solution, of the problems of the student of story, for the thinking apparent in stories has limitless complications. This study can only explore some of the most important features of this thinking.

A striking feature is that a single person about whom the hero is thinking may appear as many characters, and, conversely, several people may be embodied in one character. There are not nearly so many people involved in *The King of the Golden Mountain* as there appear to be, and they turn out to be only the protagonist himself and a very few other people about whom he is thinking.

30

As he thinks, on the level of fantasy, the hero disguises his thoughts, even from himself. The hero of *The King of the Golden Mountain* is not aware that the dwarf is an aspect of himself, embodying feelings which he, in his acknowledged form, has disowned. The hero journeys through his story as if he were performing a ritual, satisfied with the most irrational arrangements, and creating elaborate forms through which to enact and re-enact his preoccupations. The characters are part of the pictorial language through which he expresses the feelings which he experiences at each particular moment of the story. Kingship has no political reality: it is an image depicting certain thoughts of the hero. He will be a dwarf, a king, a shepherd and then a king again, according as to how he is feeling about himself; and, for the same reason, other people in the hero's thoughts appear in shifting and often extraordinary guises. Magical thinking is ubiquitous: the hero's thoughts all become deeds and events at once, while he has ways of reversing the effects of these thoughts, so that the deeds can be undone and events cancelled out. The conflict of omnipotent wishes propels the story, and is the main source of the excitement and fear.

The hero is in disguise; he is a displacement for those of us who decide to join him in his story. However, it appears that we need further disguises in order to defend ourselves from a disturbing realization of what is actually taking place. If we do not have the defences, and thus do realize the full import of the story, most of us would lose the freedom to exercise our feelings with abandon. The fun could even become a nightmare, if we become frightened by the expression of our feelings. Displacement itself is often further employed to deepen a disguise, making other vital characters in a story appear to be different people. The princess is such a displacement in *The King of the Golden Mountain*.

Apart from the complex defences already observed in the stories and dreams, there may also be defence by rationalization in stories. This activity is on the part of the intellect, not the fantasy, and, by making sure that there is a logic, which the intellect can grasp, in the story, it acts by making us feel satisfied at finding what we believe to be the 'meaning'. This gives us a comfortable feeling that we can disregard those parts of the story outside this logic as 'mere fancy'. A story may also be explained away at its beginning or end, or it may be given a moral, which can help to cancel out[2] its major purposes.

It has become clear, from the examples given of stories and dreams, that the defences are not, as their name suggests, merely protective mechanisms which enable us to avoid fear and guilt. They are in themselves a source of great enjoyment. Fun is the chief purpose of story and all the powers of the fantasy, of which the defences are a product, are bent towards this purpose. It is exhilarating to be able to create a situation where one has full scope for hating, without interference from feelings of love, and vice versa. The splendid images for which the defences are partly responsible are also a delight of dreams and stories.

When one takes up a position in the hero's mind, and experiences the story as the hero oneself, one discovers that every aspect of the story springs into significance as an essential part of a deeply meaningful whole. But there may not be only one meaning or even only two; many may be present together in the complex and delicately poised story. There will often be more than one viewpoint from which the story may be seen, for, while the acknowledged hero is the creator of the story, he may split himself up into two or more characters, or groups of characters. In many stories the hero appears in more than one acknowledged form: audiences are happy to make two, or even several, characters their representatives in the story. Varying acknowledged feelings are richly expressed by these means. Commonly in these stories the hero's rôle is played by a pair, or group, of brothers or sisters, one sometimes taking prominence over the others.[3] More difficult to observe are the hero's unacknowledged forms, through which he expresses feelings which he denies as being his own.

This study has made clear the importance of studying stories in isolation from each other. It now seems to be certain that every small incident in a story is significant and that this significance depends entirely on the particular context of the incident in its particular story. The whole sequence of incidents must also be viewed as the creation of the protagonist of that particular story. Every story must therefore be studied individually, and the use of analogy can only bring about misleading results.

It is now time to make a further study of the kinds of thinking to be found in stories. The different processes are not easily isolated, and should ideally be studied together; but, for the purpose of analysis, they will have to be separated as far as is possible, in the following chapters.

NOTES TO CHAPTER 3

1. This quotation is the complete version of the story of *The King of the Golden Mountain* as it appears in the following edition: Jacob and Wilhelm Grimm, *Grimm's Fairy Tales*, translated by Edgar Taylor (1823), (Oxford, 1962).

This is one of a large number of translations of the collection of folktales made by the Brothers Grimm, which first appeared in the following edition: *Kinder- und Haus-Märchen. Gesammelt durch die Brüder Grimm* (Berlin, 1812–15). 2 vols.

The Grimm brothers' version will not be the only version extant at the time during which they made their collection; there will have been at least slight variations. See J. Bolte and G. Polivka, *Anmerkungen zu den Kinder- und Hausmärchen der Brüder Grimm* (Liepzig, 1912–32), 5 vols. Further research into the different versions of particular stories in relation to fundamental meaning needs to be undertaken, but it cannot be undertaken here.

The following German edition may be consulted: *Die Kinder- und Hausmärchen der Brüder Grimm*, vollständige ausgabe in der urfassung, herausgegeban von Friedrich Panzer (Wiesbaden, *c*. 1950). In this edition, our story is *Der König von Goldenen Berg*, p. 372 following. It describes the dwarf simply as 'ein kleines schwarzes Männchen' and the men as 'zwölf Männer, schwarz und mit Ketten behangen'. Our 'Heads off!' appears more logically as 'Kopf alle runter, nur meiner nicht!'

The edition of *Grimm's Fairy Tales* published by Routledge & Kegan Paul (1948), which is a revision by James Stern of Margaret Hunt's translation, translates these German words more faithfully than does our version, but the deviations in our version are interesting, especially in that they show no deviation from the fundamental meaning of the story. In the Routledge & Kegan Paul edition, the story is given its standard number, 92.

2. Norman N. Holland, *The Dynamics of Literary Response* (New York, 1968), p. 54.

3. Good examples of this phenomenon are Hansel and Gretel; Snow-White and Rose-Red (No. 161 in the Grimm collection); the 'Two Brothers' (No. 60 in the Grimm collection), and the romance heroes Amis and Amiloun, and Eger and Grime, who are friends sworn in brotherhood to each other.

4   *Disguises*

DISGUISE IS OFTEN quite simple. It may comprise no more
than the assumption of the guise of animals, as in the stories of Brer
Rabbit and Brer Fox, and the animal stories of Africa from whence
these American stories spring. Kalulu the Hare and Fisi the Hyena
in the folktales of Malawi, are enacting the conflicts of African
villagers, the little hare always outwitting his more powerful neigh-
bours, as does Brer Rabbit. Anything may happen, provided that
the characters are not the human beings which they so obviously
are. As for who these human beings are, it is not disagreeable for us
to recognize our identification with the little hero; we may easily do
so.

Disguise, on the other hand, can also be a deep and complex
arrangement, with a great deal hiding behind it.

In this chapter, three stories will be studied so that the varied
characteristics of disguise may be investigated further. The stories
chosen are *Cat-Skin* and *The Golden Bird* from the Grimm collection, and the medieval romance of *Tristan*.

Cat-Skin appears as *Allerleirauh* in German editions of the folktales collected by the Brothers Grimm, and in some English translations. There are other versions of the story, including *Donkey Skin*
in Charles Perrault's collection and the medieval romance of
Emare. The version to be studied here[1] is as follows:

CAT-SKIN

There was once a King, whose Queen had hair of the purest
gold, and was so beautiful that her match was not to be met
with on the whole face of the earth. But this beautiful Queen
fell ill, and when she felt that her end drew near, she called the
King to her and said, 'Vow to me that you will never marry
again, unless you meet with a wife who is as beautiful as I am,
and who has golden hair like mine.' Then when the King in his
grief had vowed all she asked, she shut her eyes and died. But
the King was not to be comforted, and for a long time never
thought of taking another wife. At last, however, his counsellors said, 'This will not do; the King must marry again, that we

may have a Queen.' So messengers were sent far and wide, to seek for a bride who was as beautiful as the late Queen. But there was no princess in the world so beautiful; and if there had been, still there was not one to be found who had such golden hair. So the messengers came home and had done all their work for nothing.

Now the King had a daughter who was just as beautiful as her mother, and had the same golden hair. And when she had grown up, the King looked at her and saw that she was just like his late Queen: then he said to his courtiers, 'May I not marry my daughter? She is the very image of my dead wife: unless I have her, I shall not find any bride upon the whole earth, and you say there must be a Queen.' When the courtiers heard this, they were shocked, and said, 'Heaven forbid that a father should marry his daughter! Out of so great a sin no good can come.' And his daughter was also shocked, but hoped the King would soon give up such thoughts: so she said to him, 'Before I marry any one I must have three dresses; one must be of gold like the sun, another must be of shining silver like the moon, and a third must be dazzling as the stars: besides this, I want a mantle of a thousand different kinds of fur put together, to which every beast in the kingdom must give a part of his skin.' And thus she thought he would think of the matter no more. But the King made the most skilful workmen in his kingdom weave the three dresses, one as golden as the sun, another as silvery as the moon, and a third shining like the stars; and his hunters were told to hunt out all the beasts in his kingdom and take the finest fur out of their skins: and so a mantle of a thousand furs was made.

When all was ready, the King sent them to her; but she got up in the night when all were asleep, and took three of her trinkets, a golden ring, a golden necklace, and a golden brooch; and packed the three dresses of the sun, moon, and stars, up in a nutshell, and wrapped herself up in the mantle of all sorts of fur, and besmeared her face and hands with soot. Then she threw herself upon Heaven for help in her need, and went away and journeyed on the whole night, till at last she came to a large wood. As she was very tired, she sat herself down in the hollow of a tree and soon fell asleep: and there she slept on till it was midday: and it happened, that as the King to whom the wood belonged was hunting in it, his dogs came to the tree, and began to snuff about and run round and round, and then to bark. 'Look sharp,' said the King to the huntsmen, 'and see what sort of game lies there.' And the huntsmen went up to the tree, and when they came back again said, 'In the hollow tree there lies a most wonderful beast, such as we never saw before; its skin seems of a thousand kinds of fur, but there it lies fast asleep.' 'See,' said the King, 'if you can catch it alive, and we will take it with us.' So the huntsmen took it up, and the maiden awoke and was greatly frightened, and said, 'I am a poor child that has neither father nor mother left; have pity on me and take me with you.' Then they said, 'Yes, Miss Cat-Skin, you will do for the kitchen; you can sweep up the ashes and do things of that sort.' So they put her in the coach and took her home to the King's palace. Then they showed her a little corner under the staircase where no light of day ever peeped in, and said, 'Cat-Skin, you may lie and sleep there.' And she was sent into the kitchen, and made to fetch wood and water, to blow the fire, pluck the poultry, pick the herbs, sift the ashes, and do all the dirty work.

Thus Cat-Skin lived for a long time very sorrowfully. 'Ah, pretty Princess,' thought she, 'what will now become of thee!' But it happened one day that a feast was to be held in the King's castle; so she said to the cook, 'May I go up a little while and see what is going on? I will take care and stand behind the door.' And the cook said, 'Yes, you may go, but be back again in half an hour's time to rake out the ashes.' Then she took her little lamp, and went into her cabin, and took off the fur-skin, and washed the soot from off her face and hands, so that her beauty shone forth like the sun from behind the clouds. She next opened her nutshell, and brought out of it the dress that shone like the sun, and so went to the feast. Every one made way for her, for nobody knew her, and they thought she could be no less than a king's daughter. But the King came up to her and held out his hand and danced with her, and he thought in his heart, 'I never saw any one half so beautiful.'

When the dance was at an end, she curtsied; and when the King looked round for her, she was gone, no one knew whither. The guards who stood at the castle gate were called in; but they had seen no one. The truth was that she had run into her little cabin, pulled off her dress, blacked her face and hands, put on the fur-skin cloak, and was Cat-Skin again. When she went into the kitchen to her work, and began to rake the ashes, the cook said, 'Let that alone till the morning, and heat the King's soup; I should like to run up now and give a peep; but take care you don't let a hair fall into it, or you will run a chance of never eating again.'

As soon as the cook went away, Cat-Skin heated the King's soup and toasted up a slice of bread as nicely as ever she could; and when it was ready, she went and looked in the cabin for her little golden ring, and put it into the dish in which the soup was. When the dance was over, the King ordered his soup to be brought in, and it pleased him so well, that he thought he had never tasted any so good before. At the bottom he saw a gold ring lying, and as he could not make out how it had got there, he ordered the cook to be sent for. The cook was frightened when he heard the order, and said to Cat-Skin, 'You must have let a hair fall into the soup; if it be so, you will have a good beating.' Then he went before the King, who asked who had cooked the soup. 'I did,' answered the cook. But the King said, 'That is not true; it was better done than you could do it.' Then the cook answered, 'To tell the truth, I did not cook it, but Cat-Skin did.' 'Then let Cat-Skin come up,' said the King: and when she came, he said to her, 'Who are you?' 'I am a poor child,' said she, 'who has lost both father and mother.' 'How came you in my palace?' asked he. 'I am good for nothing,' said she, 'but to be scullion girl, and to have boots and shoes thrown at my head.' 'But how did you get the ring that was in the soup?' asked the King. But she would not own that she knew anything about the ring; so the King sent her away again about her business.

After a time there was another feast, and Cat-Skin asked the cook to let her go up and see it as before. 'Yes,' said he, 'but come back again in half an hour, and cook the King the soup that he likes so much.' Then she ran to her little cabin, washed herself quickly, and took the dress out which was silvery as the moon, and put it on; and when she went in looking like a king's daughter, the King went up to her and rejoiced at seeing her again, and when the dance began, he danced with her. After the dance was at an end, she managed to slip out so slyly that the King did not see where she was gone; but she sprang into her little cabin and made herself into Cat-Skin again, and went into the kitchen to cook the soup. Whilst the cook was above, she got the golden necklace, and dropped it into the soup; then it was brought to the King, who ate it, and it pleased him as well as before; so he sent for the cook, who was again forced to tell him that Cat-Skin had cooked it. Cat-Skin was brought again before the King; but she still told him that she was only fit to have the boots and shoes thrown at her head.

But when the King had ordered a feast to be got ready for the third time, it happened just the same as before. 'You must be a witch, Cat-Skin,' said the cook; 'for you always put something into the soup, so that it pleases the King better than mine.' However, he let her go up as before. Then she put on the dress which sparkled like the stars, and went into the ball-room in it; and the King danced with her again, and thought she had never looked so beautiful as she did then: so whilst he was dancing with her, he put a gold ring on her finger without her seeing it, and ordered that the dance should be kept up a long time. When it was at an end, he would have held her fast by the hand; but she slipped away and sprang so quickly through the crowd that he lost sight of her; and she ran as fast as she could into her little cabin under the stairs. But this time she kept away too long, and stayed beyond the half-hour; so she had not time to take off her fine dress, but threw her fur mantle over it, and in her haste did not soot herself all over, but left one finger white.

Then she ran into the kitchen, and cooked the King's soup; and as soon as the cook was gone, she put the golden brooch into the dish. When the King got to the bottom, he ordered Cat-Skin to be called once more, and soon saw the white finger and the ring that he had put on it whilst they were dancing: so he seized her hand, and kept fast hold of it, and when she wanted to loose herself and spring away, the fur cloak fell off a little on one side, and the starry dress sparkled underneath it. Then he got hold of the fur and tore it off, and her golden hair and beautiful form were seen, and she could no longer hide herself: so she washed the soot and ashes from off her face, and showed herself to be the most beautiful Princess upon the face of the earth. But the King said, 'You are my beloved bride, and we will never more be parted from each other.' And the wedding-feast was held, and a merry day it was.

This has not been as popular a story as many, and one reason for this must be its inadequate disguise. The open expression of an incestuous wish comes as a slight shock. However, the story does make use of disguise, and this becomes apparent when the story is approached as Cat-Skin's creation. If the initial situation in the story is seen as presented to us by Cat-Skin, who is making it appear as she wishes it to appear, it begins to make more sense. She arranges that she should be seen as a replacement for her mother, and that her father should so wish to make her Queen that he has the garments which she desires made for her. Why should she then run away? The reason must be that she has opposite wishes, those which, in part, lie behind her very arrangement of disguises.

The next part of the story, if viewed from the outside, might seem even more illogical. Why does Cat-Skin dress up in the fur mantle, and smear herself in soot, taking with her her three wonderful dresses packed in a nutshell? How strange that only a night's walk

38

away, she should come into the territory of another king. Why should she be disguised at the court of the second king? The dresses worn for his benefit were made for her by her father, in order that she should marry him. Cat-Skin deliberately courts the second king with the use of the attributes expressing her sense of her right to be Queen. The story becomes logical if Cat-Skin is seen as using the disguise of displacement here, exchanging her king father for another king.

It should not be assumed that the story is therefore disguising no more than an incestuous wish. The beautiful dresses and the fur mantle, together with the soot disguise and the heroine's adopted name, suggest that this is a complex story, expressing a number of conflicting feelings. In the midst of all her feelings, the heroine seems to be reaching out for a sense of her own splendour.

The story is remarkable for its sense of play, which attracts and disarms the reader at every point. The heroine's plans take form like a ceremonial dance, one of the many purposes of which may be to distract attention from the exact nature of some of the feelings achieving expression.

In *Cat-Skin* are apparent many important facets of the thought-processes which create stories, and there will be further references to it in succeeding chapters. The main features of its disguises do not, themselves, require so much analysis and discussion as do those in the next story, *The Golden Bird*.[2] Once again, the story is short enough to quote in full:

THE GOLDEN BIRD

A certain king had a beautiful garden, and in the garden stood a tree which bore golden apples. These apples were always counted, and about the time when they began to grow ripe it was found that every night one of them was gone. The King became very angry at this, and ordered the gardener to keep watch all night under the tree. The gardener set his eldest son to watch; but about twelve o'clock he fell asleep, and in the morning another of the apples was missing. Then the second son was ordered to watch; and at midnight he too fell asleep, and in the morning another apple was gone. Then the third son offered to keep watch; but the gardener at first would not let him, for fear some harm should come to him: however, at last he consented, and the young man laid himself under the tree to watch. As the clock struck twelve he heard a rustling noise in the air, and a bird came flying that was of pure gold; and as it was snapping at one of the apples with its beak, the gardener's son jumped up and shot an arrow at it. But the arrow did the

39

bird no harm; only it dropped a golden feather from its tail, and then flew away. The golden feather was brought to the King in the morning, and all the council was called together. Everyone agreed that it was worth more than all the wealth of the kingdom: but the King said, 'One feather is of no use to me; I must have the whole bird.'

Then the gardener's eldest son set out and thought to find the golden bird very easily; and when he had gone but a little way, he came to a wood, and by the side of the wood he saw a fox sitting; so he took his bow and made ready to shoot at it. Then the fox said, 'Do not shoot me, for I will give you good counsel; I know what your business is, and that you want to find the golden bird. You will reach a village in the evening; and when you get there, you will see two inns opposite each other, one of which is very pleasant and beautiful to look at: go not in there, but rest for the night in the other, though it may appear to you to be very poor and mean.' But the son thought to himself, 'What can such a beast as this know about the matter?' So he shot his arrow at the fox; but he missed it, and it set up its tail above its back and ran into the wood. Then he went his way, and in the evening came to the village where the two inns were; and in one of these were people singing, and dancing, and feasting; but the other looked very dirty, and poor. 'I should be very silly,' said he, 'if I went to that shabby house, and left this charming place;' so he went into the smart house, and ate and drank at his ease, and forgot the bird, and his country too.

Time passed on; and as the eldest son did not come back, and no tidings were heard of him, the second son set out, and the same thing happened to him. He met the fox, who gave him the same good advice: but when he came to the two inns, his eldest brother was standing at the window where the merrymaking was, and called to him to come in; and he could not withstand the temptation, but went in, and forgot the golden bird and his country in the same manner.

Time passed on again, and the youngest son too wished to set out into the wide world to seek for the golden bird; but his father would not listen to him for a long while, for he was very fond of his son, and was afraid that some ill luck might happen to him also, and prevent his coming back. However, at last it was agreed he should go, for he would not rest at home; and as he came to the wood, he met the fox, and heard the same good counsel. But he was thankful to the fox, and did not attempt his life as his brothers had done; so the fox said, 'Sit upon my tail, and you will travel faster.' So he sat down, and the fox began to run, and away they went over stock and stone so quick that their hair whistled in the wind.

When they came to the village, the son followed the fox's counsel, and, without looking about him, went to the shabby inn and rested there all night at his ease. In the morning came the fox again, and met him as he was beginning his journey, and said, 'Go straight forward, till you come to a castle, before which lie a whole troop of soldiers fast asleep and snoring: take no notice of them, but go into the castle and pass on and on till you come to a room, where the golden bird sits in a wooden cage. Close by it stands a beautiful golden cage, but do not try to take the bird out of the shabby cage and put it into the handsome one, otherwise you will repent it.' Then the fox stretched out his tail again, and the young man sat himself down, and away they went over stock and stone till their hair whistled in the wind.

Before the castle gate all was as the fox had said: so the son went in and found the chamber where the golden bird hung in a wooden cage, and below stood the golden cage, and the three golden apples that had been lost were lying close by it. Then thought he to himself, 'It will be a very silly thing to bring away such a fine bird in this shabby cage;' so he opened the door and took hold of it and put it into the golden cage. But the bird set up such a loud scream that all the soldiers awoke, and they took him prisoner and carried him before the King. The next morning the court sat to judge him; and when all was heard, it sentenced him to die, unless he should bring the King the golden horse which could run as swiftly as the wind; and if he did this, he was to have the golden bird given him for his own.

So he set out once more on his journey, sighing, and in great despair, when on a sudden his good friend the fox met him, and said, 'You see now what has happened on account of your not listening to my counsel. I will still, however, tell you how to find the golden horse, if you will do as I bid you. You must go straight on till you come to the castle where the horse stands in his stall: by his side will lie the groom fast asleep and snoring: take away the horse quietly, but be sure to put the old leathern saddle upon him, and not the golden one that is close by it.' Then the son sat down on the fox's tail, and away they went over stock and stone till their hair whistled in the wind.

All went right, and the groom lay snoring with his hand upon the golden saddle. But when the son looked at the horse, he thought it a great pity to put the leathern saddle upon it. 'I will give him the good one,' said he; 'I am sure he deserves it.' As he took up the golden saddle the groom awoke and cried out so loud that all the guards ran in and took him prisoner, and in the morning he was again brought before the court to be judged, and was sentenced to die. But it was agreed that, if he could bring thither the beautiful Princess, he should live, and have the bird and the horse given him for his own.

Then he went his way again very sorrowful; but the old fox came and said, 'Why did not you listen to me? If you had, you would have carried away both the bird and the horse; yet will I once more give you counsel. Go straight on, and in the evening you will arrive at a castle. At twelve o'clock at night the Princess goes to the bathing-house: go up to her and give her a kiss, and she will let you lead her away; but take care you do not suffer her to go and take leave of her father and mother.' Then the fox stretched out his tail, and so away they went over stock and stone till their hair whistled again.

As they came to the castle, all was as the fox had said, and at twelve o'clock the young man met the Princess going to the bath and gave her the kiss, and she agreed to run away with him, but begged with many tears that he would let her take leave of her father. At first he refused, but she wept still more and more, and fell at his feet, till at last he consented; but the moment she came to her father's house, the guards awoke and he was taken prisoner again.

Then he was brought before the King, and the King said, 'You shall never have my daughter unless in eight days you dig away the hill that stops the view from my window.' Now this hill was so big that the whole world could not take it away: and when he had worked for seven days, and had done very little, the fox came and said, 'Lie down and go to sleep; I will work for you.' And in the morning he awoke and the hill was gone; so he went merrily to the King, and told him that now that it was removed he must give him the Princess.

Then the King was obliged to keep his word, and away went the young man and the Princess; and the fox came and said to him, 'We will have all three, the Princess, the horse, and the bird.' 'Ah!' said the young man, 'that would be a great thing, but how can you contrive it?'

'If you will only listen,' said the fox, 'it can soon be done. When you come to the King, and he asks for the beautiful Princess, you must say, "Here she is!" Then he will be very joyful; and you will mount the golden horse that they are to give you, and put out your hand to take leave of them; but shake hands with the Princess last. Then lift her quickly on to the horse behind you; clap your spurs to his side, and gallop away as fast as you can.'

All went right: then the fox said, 'When you come to the castle where the bird is, I will stay with the Princess at the door, and you will ride in and speak to the King; and when he sees that it is the right horse, he will bring out the bird; but you must sit still, and say that you want to look at it, to see whether it is the true golden bird; and when you get it into your hand, ride away.'

This, too, happened as the fox said; they carried off the bird, the Princess mounted again, and they rode on to a great wood. Then the fox came, and said, 'Pray kill me, and cut off my head and my feet.' But the young man refused to do it: so the fox said, 'I will at any rate give you good counsel: beware of two things; ransom no one from the gallows, and sit down by the side of no river.' Then away he went. 'Well,' thought the young man, 'it is no hard matter to keep that advice.'

He rode on with the Princess, till at last he came to the village where he had left his two brothers. And there he heard a great noise and uproar; and when he asked what was the matter, the people said, 'Two men are going to be hanged.' As he came nearer, he saw that the two men were his brothers, who had turned robbers; so he said, 'Cannot they in any way be saved?' But the people said, 'No', unless he would bestow all his money upon the rascals and buy their liberty. Then he did not stay to think about the matter, but paid what was asked, and his brothers were given up, and went on with him towards their home.

And as they came to the wood where the fox first met them, it was so cool and pleasant that the two brothers said, 'Let us sit down by the side of the river, and rest a while, to eat and drink.' So he said, 'Yes', and forgot the fox's counsel, and sat down on the side of the river; and while he suspected nothing, they came behind, and threw him down the bank, and took the Princess, the horse, and the bird, and went home to the King their master, and said, 'All this have we won by our labour.' Then there was great rejoicing made; but the horse would not eat, the bird would not sing, and the Princess wept.

The youngest son fell to the bottom of the river-bed: luckily it was nearly dry, but his bones were almost broken, and the bank was so steep that he could find no way to get out. Then the old fox came once more, and scolded him for not following his advice; otherwise no evil would have befallen him. 'Yet,' said he, 'I cannot leave you here, so lay hold of my tail and hold fast.' Then he pulled him out of the river, and said to him,

43

as he got upon the bank, 'Your brothers have set watch to kill you, if they find you in the kingdom.' So he dressed himself as a poor man, and came secretly to the King's court, and was scarcely within the doors when the horse began to eat, and the bird to sing, and the Princess left off weeping. Then he went to the King, and told him all his brothers' roguery; and they were seized and punished, and he had the Princess given to him again; and after the King's death he was heir to his kingdom.

A long while after, he went to walk one day in the wood, and the old fox met him, and besought him with tears in his eyes to kill him, and cut off his head and feet. And at last he did so, and in a moment the fox was changed into a man, and turned out to be the brother of the Princess, who had been lost a great many many years.

A danger of the argument that stories are disguised is that the suggestion that nothing is what it seems can be used in an attempt to prove anything which one may wish to prove. The first step in getting to grips with what is actually happening in a story is to experience it feelingly, as do audiences. Then one must ask oneself questions about one's experience. Who is the hero of *The Golden Bird*? With whom do we identify at each stage of the story? We experience the adventures with the youngest son, the fox, and, at times, with the two elder brothers. The acknowledged hero is the youngest son: it is he who creates the story, and he has chosen to appear in disguise in other characters, who must therefore be expressing aspects of his thoughts which he wishes both to express and to disown.

Further important methods of disguise are also employed. This story, like that of *Cat-Skin*, is highly formalized, and its formality, combined with its conventionally attractive imagery, helps to hide that which is actually taking place. In fact, it is only when one reaches the final words of the story that one has any clear idea as to the nature of the activities recounted in it, and, even then, one can only achieve this if one realizes that the fox is the hero himself. It is only because the fox is thoroughly split off from himself that the hero dare state that he is really the brother of the princess whom the hero has married. The fox is so successful a disguise that the full force of the revelation does not strike the conscious mind.

Apart from splitting himself up, the hero has taken the further precaution of splitting up the 'kings' into four. This disguise wears a little thin at the end of the story, where there is a revealing confusion as to which 'king' the hero becomes heir to: it is apparent that the hero hardly cares about the maintenance of this disguise. The splitting up of the kings has all been part of the hero's formalized plan for his story, a plan which adds greatly to its fun as well as to its ability to avert our attention from that which is actually taking place. This is a deeply disguised story; it would be impossible to penetrate the disguises with any sense of conviction, were it not for the final words.

It is apparent that the hero postpones the final words until he feels that he has taken every precaution. It is interesting that he regards them as essential. The precursor to them comes after we have enjoyed the ritual of the golden apples in the king's garden, the golden bird, the golden horse, the hill and the princess, coming as they do within a pattern of pleasing repetition, the fox and the hero travelling from king to king 'over stock and stone till their hair whistled in the wind'. Superficially this imparts such satisfaction that when it is over, and the hero has the bird, the horse and the princess in his possession, it comes as a surprise that the fox breaks the harmony with his request: 'Pray kill me, and cut off my head and my feet'. This is a measure of the success of the story up till now, but once one has stopped to think, one can see that the hero may well have much to come to terms with. At the end of the delightful ritual the acknowledged hero feels splendid, but while he is deeply aware of himself in the fox this feeling cannot last. The fox is desperately in need of a resolution, and therefore the story must continue in search of it, on a rather different note.

The hero decides to make use of the two elder brothers to prepare the way. He already has a wish to eliminate all that these brothers represent. They are that aspect of himself which has been incapable of achieving the golden bird, the golden horse and the princess. They have no splendour. Now they are suddenly turned into robbers and murderers, stealing the hero's gains and seeking to get rid of him. When the hero tells the king what they have done, they are punished, and the hero receives back his princess. He will succeed the king after his death.

Until the elder brothers are turned into thieves, the only thefts which we hear of are those perpetrated by the youngest son and the fox, at the fox's instigation—apart, of course, from those of the golden bird, which the brothers did not see. Now the hero proclaims the brothers as the thieves who steal the bird, the horse and the princess, and he reports this to the king, who punishes the brothers and exalts the acknowledged hero. All this is apparently a contrivance by which the hero makes a disguised confession and arranges for the thefts to be punished, while his acknowledged self is acclaimed. Thus he achieves the sense that he has made all aboveboard and been forgiven by the king whom he has robbed. He also disposes of his thieving aspect in the brothers.

This does not bring about the essential resolution, however, or the story would end here. The hero thinks of the fox weeping and begging to be killed, beheaded and mutilated. These are punitive actions and suggestive of the crime for which the fox is to be punished. The hero is still reluctant, but at last agrees to obey his fox's request. Another perfomance of confession and punishment takes place, but this time in the reverse order of punishment, followed by confession. The confession is masked by the deepest disguise and the whole scene is represented as taking place alone in a forest, not before a king. The hero has delayed this scene until after he has cleared everything to his satisfaction with the king and acclaimed himself wholly forgiven by this all-powerful figure. When he feels that nothing will be lost by it, he faces the task of bringing about a resolution for the fox. The self-deceit at the court is not adequate when the hero is finally confronted with his vital need for self-forgiveness. The fox must undergo a punishment which fits the crime before he can feel as splendid a prince as does the hero, and there must be an actual confession, albeit in deep disguise. The hero is now making it to himself and not to the king. When all this has taken place, the hero is at peace with himself and his story ends.

As has already been mentioned, the imagery, apart from that of the characters, plays an important part in disguising the events of this story. It satisfies us completely at a superficial level by virtue of its grace and also owing to the fact that it is experienced as adequately meaningful at this level. We feel no puzzlement which leads us to wonder what it could mean, and, even now, it would seem a pity to disturb it by analysing it. There is also no longer any need to do so. The golden bird which steals the golden apples from the king's garden can be left to tell all that remains to be told of its own story. Contemplation of the golden bird, the golden horse and the princess in the context of the story, with detailed investigation of the way in which the hero first fails to attain them and then succeeds, will, in time, reveal hitherto hidden significance. They are, above all, attributes of 'kingship', the state to which the hero aspires, and his success in attaining them begins when his fox-self succeeds in removing the hill which offends the king. All these images have perplexing multiple significance.

The romance of *Tristan*[3] is the final story chosen for this investigation of disguises. The events of this famous medieval story are as follows:

Rivalin, lord of Parmenie, makes an enemy of Duke Morgan by riding into his land and taking towns and fortresses. After this, the two lords are constantly attacking each other. Then Rivalin goes on a pleasure trip to the court of King Mark of Cornwall, enjoying a festival there and falling in love with the king's sister Blancheflor. She also loves him and they languish with love for each other until Rivalin is seriously wounded in battle, while fighting an enemy of

46

King Mark. As he lies ill, Blancheflor comes to him and they make love. This love saves Rivalin from death and, at the same time, a son is conceived. Meanwhile, however, Morgan has attacked Parmenie and Rivalin must go home quickly. Blancheflor secretly sails away with him, but their marriage ends in the death of Rivalin as he battles against Morgan. Blancheflor dies of grief and her baby, Tristan, is therefore given a name which means sorrow.

Tristan is brought up by a faithful steward Rual, until he is abducted by Norwegian sailors and thus crosses the channel to Cornwall. There he arrives at the court of King Mark, who is his mother's brother. Neither realize their relationship, until Rual arrives to make it known, but the hero makes a great impression on the king. After Rual's revelations, Tristan is knighted and he then wishes to avenge his father. He sails home, slays Morgan in a forest and then returns to King Mark. Next, he becomes involved in single combat against his uncle's enemy King Morold on an island. During this combat, Tristan is given a wound in the thigh, and is told by King Morold that this can only be healed by his sister, Queen Isolde of Ireland. Tristan then slays Morold, in spite of his wound, by striking him on the head in such a way that a fragment of his sword is left in the king's skull. Once again, he crosses water and this time he arrives in disguise as a minstrel called Tantris. Queen Isolde heals him of the wound which, by this time, has a vile odour, and Tantris wins the hearts of the queen and her daughter, also Isolde, with his harping. Returning, fully recovered, to King Mark's court, Tristan tells his uncle about the queen's daughter, the fair young Isolde. He lyrically describes the princess's exquisite beauty and charm as if he were her lover. Meanwhile, King Mark's councillors are urging him to marry and beget an heir and, at first, Mark replies that there is no need for he has Tristan. But these men hate Tristan, call him a sorcerer and wish to destroy him. Believing that their ends would be secured if Tristan is sent to Ireland to ask for the hand of Princess Isolde, on behalf of King Mark, they suggest this to the king. The king's interest in the princess has already been roused by Tristan's praise of her, but he realizes the danger to Tristan if he should lead the embassy, and recognizes the wicked intent of his councillors. However, Tristan overrules him, for he wishes to go. This time, he arrives in Ireland disguised as a merchant, and he finds that the country is in the power of a fearsome dragon. The king of Ireland has sworn that he will give his daughter to the man who slays it, and Tristan succeeds in doing so, alone and unseen. A steward finds the dragon dead and claims to be its slayer, unchallenged by Tristan, who is unconscious after his battle. It is soon discovered that the slayer is not the steward but 'Tantris', who is healed again by Queen Isolde. She diagnoses his illness as being due to the fumes from the dragon's tongue, which the hero has cut off and taken. Meanwhile, Princess Isolde begins to realize that Tantris is Tristan and she proves it by matching the fragment of his sword, which had been found in her uncle Morold's head, with his sword, which was damaged in that combat. The princess wishes to kill the hero, but it is eventually agreed that he should live, and he then makes known King Mark's suit. It is accepted, and Tristan and Princess Isolde set sail for England with Brangane, Isolde's maid. During the voyage Tristan and Isolde mistakenly drink the magic love potion which Queen Isolde had made up for her daughter and King Mark, and entrusted to Brangane. This is how it comes about that Tristan and Isolde fall hopelessly in love for ever. Isolde marries King Mark, but she has a life-long love-affair with Tristan, even when he is also married—to yet another Isolde. He cannot consummate his marriage with this third Isolde, because his loved Isolde's ring, given to him as a token, reminds him of her love.

There are many events in the story of the years between the drinking of the potion and the death of the lovers, and it is clear from the different surviving versions of the story, and Marie de France's short lay, *Lai De Chevrefoil*,[4] that many imaginations played with these years. The servant Brangane is substituted for Isolde on Mark's wedding night, so that the king might think his bride a virgin. Later, when Mark knows about his wife's unfaithfulness, many adventures take place, the most famous of which are the ordeal by oath, when the lovers trick Mark into believing that Isolde is true to him, and the lovers' year of banishment in a forest. They are found there by Mark, who sees them asleep in a cave with a naked sword between them, which is interpreted mistakenly to be a sign of their chastity. Tristan also kills a giant who wants the beard of the king whom he is serving in Spain, and he overcomes another giant who consequently helps him to make a hall in a cave, full of statues of Isolde, Brangane and others, such as the dwarf who had revealed to Mark that Tristan and Isolde were meeting secretly. When Tristan's brother-in-law Caerdin sees the statue of Brangane, he desires her and joins the hero in a secret meeting with the women, from which they have to flee because enemies hear of it. Brangane feels ashamed and tells Mark that Isolde is having an affair with Cariado, the enemy who discovered the affair and mocked Caerdin's cowardice. In order to see Isolde, Tristan resorts to the disguises of a pilgrim and a leper, and, in his last adventure, he is struck by a poisoned spear in the loins as he helps a man called 'Dwarf Tristan' to regain his stolen wife. Dwarf Tristan is killed and Tristan himself is mortally wounded. He sends for Isolde and she sets sail at once, but her voyage is delayed by a storm.

When her ship is sighted, Tristan's wife tells Tristan that the sail is black, indicating that Isolde is not coming to him. Tristan feels greater pain than he has ever felt, for only Isolde can heal him, and he dies for love of her, saying that she has no pity for him but that he takes solace in the thought that she will grieve over his death. Isolde arrives too late to heal him of his wounds, and, embracing him, remains in that embrace as she dies for him in return.

This apparently rambling, and yet haunting, story can be seen to have organic, coherent form if it is approached as being a series of thoughts in the mind of the hero, represented by a multiplicity of images. The fragmentation of characters and of feelings will only partly be for purposes of disguise: it will also be owing to a wish to simplify complex matters and to express them in vivid images with which the protagonist can play. Once one enters this story as Tristan, one finds that his concern to disguise his thoughts is not always a prime concern. He uses the same name, Isolde, for three of his women characters, and calls another character 'Dwarf Tristan'. Thus the romance of Tristan provided this study with its first clues as to what is taking place in stories.

The hero begins his story as Rivalin who initiates hostilities against Morgan and falls in love with Blanchflor, sister to King Mark. The love is all longing until the hero is wounded in a battle against an enemy of King Mark. He fights the rival in himself, suffering injury, but also achieving, as a result, union with the woman he loves. This restores him to health and he secretly steals his love away as he, at the same time, visualizes himself as facing renewed attacks from 'Duke Morgan'. These attacks are to be fatal; the union between the hero and his love ends in death, just at the time when the life of Tristan, conceived at the first love-making, begins. The hero felt that his dream must end, but after this sorrow and death he renews it, abandoning his more explicit name for one of grief.

Continuing his story as Tristan, the hero's feelings are the same as they were when he was Rivalin, but he now explores them in much greater detail, and the reasons for the sorrow and the death become clearer. He sees himself first as in the care of a loving, humble father Rual, whose situation is no threat to himself, and then, when he is a youth, he transfers himself to the court of a powerful uncle, King Mark. Here he is well-received and, later, recognized. Then he slays Morgan, his father's killer. After this, he slays King Morold by giving him a blow on the head with his sword, leaving a fragment of the sword in Morold's skull. But Morold has already given him a wound in the thigh which can only be healed by his sister, Queen Isolde. In Morold, the hero has created a mutilating father whom he destroys, but there is a suggestion that he has damaged himself sexually in doing so. Meanwhile, he has already arranged for a more drastic injury of this kind given him by a king which can only be healed by a queen who is the king's sister. In order to be healed by the queen, he has, as the slayer of the king, to be in disguise. As a minstrel he enjoys the healing of a wound, which is described as disgusting, in the care of a healing mother and a beautiful girl, her daughter. They both have the same name. After this incident, Tristan arranges the marriage between King Mark and Isolde the daughter. He visualizes himself as Mark's beloved heir who is to be ousted, and the girl whom he admires is not to be his wife, but King Mark's. He, as the slayer of King Morold, cannot reveal himself as an eligible suitor for Isolde and, so far in his story, he admits no love for her. Penetrating the disguises in this part of the story, it is possible to see that Tristan's basic problem is that he cannot dissociate Isolde the daughter, a desirable and eligible wife, from Isolde the mother, whom he also desires. Isolde is taboo; she belongs to another man, and therefore can never belong to the hero. She belongs to a 'king': the hero's father, King Morold and King Mark. This is why he cannot arrange to marry her, and marries her to his 'uncle' instead.

The story of Tristan appears to be the story of the eternal sadness associated with the hero's having to renounce his maternal first love. Indeed, he has been unable to renounce the sexual side of his love for her in his mind and therefore embarks on a search for her which can never be satisfied in his lifetime.

This is the reason why Tristan sees his rôle as the hopeless lover, and also as the enemy and victim of fathers. There is a dragon between himself and the winning of Isolde, which expresses his conception of his love for her as monstrous and terrifying, and impossible of fulfilment, unless this monstrous and terrifying barrier of taboo is overcome. The hero wishes the barrier to be there; he put it there in order to keep himself and Isolde apart, and yet he also put it there in order to overcome it, as an attempt to declare it non-existent. In this scene, the hero pictures his rival as a mere deceitful steward, who tries to steal his rightful prize, Isolde, from him. The hero also pictures himself as cutting out the dragon's tongue and being overcome as a result.[5] Only Queen Isolde can heal him. This reveals that the hero is visualizing the dragon barrier as, in part, a father-figure, and his terror over his murderous and mutilating act can only be healed by the queen. Immediately after this, the hero visualizes the discovery of his identity as King Morold's slayer by the young Isolde. He pictures her murderous anger, but arranges for his forgiveness, sealing this by bringing up the subject of her marriage with King Mark. Tristan overcomes the dragon and yet he does not overcome the dragon. The thieving, deceitful steward is, to a certain extent, himself: this is, in part, how he sees the events which are to follow. From now on, King Mark, Isolde the daughter (who becomes 'Queen Isolde') and the hero are the chief characters of the story. Isolde the mother drops out of it, and Brangane the waiting-maid enters it. The magic potion, significantly prepared by Isolde the mother, expresses the nature of the feeling which has the hero in its grip, never to be resolved. The hero sees the magical power as coming from his mother while he is helpless. In his mind he possesses Isolde and yet she, by nature, belongs to another. He attempts a marriage with an Isolde but it fails; he cannot consummate the marriage when he thinks of Queen Isolde, and he thinks of her whenever he looks at the ring which she has given him.

Tristan's adventures during the years of the love affair express his conflicting feelings. He has possessed Isolde and yet he has not. Brangane is the unpossessed Isolde, and yet this is a trick because there is also a possessed Isolde. The ordeal by oath[6] is a similar trick expressing the truth and yet not the truth; it is fundamentally not the truth, because there cannot be an unpossessed Isolde for the hero, while he possesses her in his mind. This is also the case in the sword-in-the-forest scene.[7] A sword between a couple was a sign of chastity, for it kept them apart, and yet the very imagery of the naked sword between the sleeping couple in a cave proclaims the possibility that the reverse is the truth about the time in the forest. Meanwhile the hero is haunted by the feeling that he is a low-down thief. During the episode of the ordeal, he is a disfigured pilgrim, and, later, he becomes a leper, in order to snatch a meeting with Isolde.[8] He sees himself as revealing the truth to Mark, first belittled, so that he appears as a dwarf,[9] and then through a cowardly escapade which outrages the Brangane aspect of Isolde.[10] He conceives of his sexual designs against a 'king' as a monstrous giant and slays it,[11] and later overcomes another giant in a forest, using this image of himself, subsequently, to help him make the images.[12] However, the dwarf is among them, and the shameful escapade results. At the last, he only succeeds in seeing himself as a dwarf— 'Dwarf Tristan'—whose wife has been stolen from him. This 'dwarf' appears first as a tall and stalwart knight, and it is startlingly incongruous that he should call himself a dwarf. He is finally referred to as 'Tristan the Dwarf', when he is killed trying to regain his wife from Estult l'Orgillus of Castle Fer on the outskirts of a wood. Tristan simultaneously receives a poisonous wound in the loins.[13]

Now Tristan conjures up a vision of his death, and the consequent death of his unattainable Isolde. If she is dead, this Isolde is no longer the wife of Mark and if he is dead, Tristan can deny that he has achieved eternal union with her. He can see no other way of solving his conflicts, and he can only achieve this solution with difficulty. The unattainable Isolde fails to reach him before he dies, because in his mind there is a wife and she cannot be the Isolde he loves. When he thinks of a wife, Isolde cannot be there, and so she is not there until he is dead, when it matters no longer. The hero dwells on his death scene, the scene which can become the end of his story, as the solution of his conflicts. In the words of Thomas, the hero's vision of himself as having at last achieved the unattainable woman through the power of his longing, is revealingly conveyed. She is seen as coming to him, rather than he to her, and she is tender like a mother. He is seen as receiving her love, while denying this victory by proclaiming his death:

> 'Tristans murut pur sun desir,
> Ysolt, qu'a tens n'i pout venir.
> Tristans murut pur sue amur,
> Ela bele Ysolt pur tendrur.'[14]

Far more may be discernible in these stories than is brought out by these analyses of them, for stories must be as complex as the minds which produce them, but while there may be disagreement as to what stories mean, there must be agreement as to the fact that they do mean. Every seemingly trivial detail can be seen to have meaning. There is deliberate intention in every minor aspect of a story and much of this intention is to create disguises. Fantasy-thinking seems to be irrational, but it is concerned with the reality of feelings and their conflicts, and with the reality of our need to both celebrate our feelings and resolve our conflicts. It is also concerned with the reality of our need to defend ourselves against a conscious realization of what we are feeling and doing as we create stories. We have a wish that the exact nature of our enjoyment be kept secret, hidden both from others and ourselves, in case either others or we ourselves should take away the enjoyment. If the exact nature of the enjoyment were known, it might indeed be taken from us. The disguises are essential for the survival of stories; without disguises they could not be enjoyed, and if they were not enjoyed, they would cease to exist.

1. This quotation is the complete version of the story of *Cat-Skin* as it appears in the following edition: Jacob and Wilhelm Grimm, *Grimm's Fairy Tales*, translated by Edgar Taylor (Oxford, 1962). The story has the standard number 65 in many editions although not in ours. In Friedrich Panzer's German edition (see note 1 to Chapter 3), the story is entitled *Allerlei-Rauh* and is number 65, p. 235.

It is interesting to compare the name 'Cat-Skin' with the name 'Allerleirauh' in the Grimm Brothers' collection. Some translators have chosen the name 'Cat-Skin', as a substitute for a name which has no meaning in English. The Routledge & Kegan Paul edition (see note 1 to Chapter 3) has a note explaining that Allerleirauh means 'of many different kinds of fur' (p. 326). Certainly 'allerlei' implies 'a great variety' (in an admirable sense), but in the case of 'rauh' there appears to be a play on words. 'Rauh' means 'rough', 'coarse', 'rude' and 'rauch' means 'smoke' and also, dialectally, 'soot'. 'Rauch' can also mean 'shaggy' and, in 'rauchwaren', 'rauch-werk', 'furs', 'peltry'. During the nineteenth century in Hamburg, there was an institution for homeless boys called 'Rauches Haus'. Both the names 'Allerleirauh' and 'Cat-Skin' require detailed consideration.

2. This quotation is the complete version of the story of *The Golden Bird* as it appears in the following edition: Jacob and Wilhelm Grimm, *Grimm's Fairy Tales*, translated by Edgar Taylor (Oxford, 1962). In many editions of the Grimm collection, this story has the standard number 57. In Friedrich Panzer's German edition, the story is entitled *Vom Goldnen Vogel* and is number 57, p. 208.

Edgar Taylor's translation is usually faithful to the German original, but the Routledge & Kegan Paul edition (see note 1 to Chapter 3), where the story appears as No. 57, p. 272, has altered the hero's status from that of a gardener's son to that of a king's son. In this version there is also an interesting elaboration of the end of the story, giving more importance to the final scene with the fox. It is a significant example of elaboration, revealing the translator's apprehension of the importance of this scene. These sentences are included: 'But what happened to the poor fox? Long afterwards the king's son was once again walking in the wood, when the Fox met him and said: "You have everything now that you can wish for, but there is never an end to my misery, and yet it is in your power to free me . . ." ' (*Grimm's Fairy Tales*, published by Routledge & Kegan Paul (1948), p. 279).

There is significance in every such variation. The alteration from gardener's son to king's son reveals an apprehension of meaning, discarding a disguise, and also replacing a sense of lowliness with one of princely splendour. Now that the hero is acknowledged to be son to the 'king', the fact that he is only the third son springs into greater significance and assumes greater importance in the story.

The Routledge & Kegan Paul edition is more faithful to the German original in some respects than is the translation of Edgar Taylor. It translates 'brunnen' as 'well', while Taylor gives us 'river', a variation which cannot be without significance.

3. The romance of Tristan does not survive in any one complete version, but there are a large number of fragments in medieval German, French and English, which, together, give us the complete story. The complete story in modern English may be found in A. T. Hatto's translation of the *Tristan* of Gottfried von Strassburg, supplemented by the *Tristan* of Thomas (Penguin Books, 1960), from which the story is here summarized. There is also *The Tale of Tristan's Madness* and *The Romance of Tristan* by Beroul, translated by Alan S. Fedrick (Penguin Books, 1970).

The names of the characters which this book uses are almost all those used in the *Tristan* of Gottfried von Strassburg. In English versions they are Tristrem, Isonde, Rouland (Rivalin), Rohand (Rual), Mark, Morgan, Moraunt (Morold) and Brengwain. Isolde is called Îsôt or Îsolt by Gottfried, but I have preferred to keep the familiar form Isolde.

4. *Les Lais de Marie de France*, edited by Jean Rychner (Paris, 1966).

Lays of Marie de France, translated by Eugene Mason (Everyman's Library, 1911), No. 10.

5. *Gottfried von Strassburg: Tristan*, translated by A. T. Hatto (Penguin Books), p. 161.

6. *Ibid.*, pp. 245–8.

7. *Ibid.*, pp. 270–2. Gottfried has King Mark see the ambiguity of the scene with poignant clarity, feeling pain and suspicion together with pleasure and relief. The scene ends with this judgement of his:

> ‚Schulde?‘ sprach er ‚triuwen, ja‘.
> ‚Schulde?‘ sprach er ‚triuwen, nein‘.

Gottfried von Strassburg: *Tristan und Isolde*, edited by Wolfgang Golther (Berlin and Stuttgart, 1888), 1753–5.

8. *Gottfried von Strassburg: Tristan*, translated by A. T. Hatto (Penguin Books), p. 332.

9. *Ibid.*, pp. 232–5.
10. *Ibid.*, pp. 321–31.
11. *Ibid.*, pp. 311–12.
12. *Ibid.*, pp. 315–16.
13. *Ibid.*, pp. 339–41.

14. *Les Fragments du Roman de Tristan par Thomas*, edited by Bartina H. Wind (Leiden, 1950), Fragment Sneyd, 816–19.

5 Form

IT HAS BEEN observed that, when we dream, we have certain feelings first and then we begin to think about them. This thinking is the thinking of fantasy, and the language which it uses is that of imagery. These images appear in a certain order, forming a sequence which has already been seen to have a definite logic. It is now time to consider the morphology of the sequences of images which appear in stories. That of dreams is created by the fantasy. That of stories is also created by the fantasy, but, in their case, the conscious intellect's powers of directed thinking modifies the production of fantasy and produces conscious art. This modification is essential in the shared story, because the conscious mind desires a measure of comprehension at the conscious level of the mind; otherwise it feels too confused to enjoy the story. The conscious mind also delights in order, while fantasy is happy to meander from one image to another; there is often no particular reason why a creation of fantasy should ever end.

Stories have a linear pattern of which a morphological study can be made. This is a study of a different nature from that of the tortuous patterns created by disguise, but it will be seen that each study illuminates the other. As the linear pattern of stories is created by both the thinking of fantasy and the intellect's powers of directed thinking, the nature of the activity of both in the process of creation must be under scrutiny in this chapter.

It is apparent that the forces which impel the fantasy to create a story are those of our wishes. Within the created world of the story, these wishes have omnipotence; but wishes may change, and many wishes may be present at once, conflicting with each other. Wishes cease to be all-powerful when opposite wishes intervene. Thus the story takes form in order to allow a number of different wishes to achieve expression, while, at the same time, progressing as a struggle to achieve the final triumph of certain wishes over others. The dramatic progression of the story is created, however, not only by the conflict of wishes, but also by the conflict between wishes and certain opposing feelings—such as a sense of powerlessness. The hero may even feel the need to arm his wishes with greater power by concentrating and binding the wishes in some definite, controllable form, such as a special word or object. As the story

55

progresses, the delight which fantasy takes in contrasts, and in celebrating feelings in isolation from each other, helps to create coherent form.

At the same time, the intellect is active. If a dream is to be shared, it needs to be given a formal pattern of some kind, which will capture and satisfy the conscious mind, and also be more easily remembered. Conscious art selects particular aspects of the creations of fantasy and, while remaining faithful to them, helps to give them balance and order. It also selects only a few of the limitless number of images created by the dreaming mind. While there is an unconscious linking process constantly taking place in the mind, giving rise to the private pictorial language of dreams, conscious art employs only those images which readily communicate feelings to audiences. Thus the effect of its activities is that stories are less varied, more stereotyped and more coherent than are dreams. The ritual form and memorable imagery of *Cat-Skin* and *The Golden Bird* are good examples of this: they give greater delight to the conscious mind, and a greater coherence to the events of the stories, than do the dreams which have been studied. The shared stories have concerned themselves with matters of form which were not at all necessary in the private stories of the dreams.

There is also some reference, in stories, to the realities of the outside world, so that a story does make some sense, as we contemplate it in a state of mind which is, inevitably, aware of the realities of the outer world, as well as those of our inner world. While we do suspend our disbelief, thus allowing our conscious minds to become engaged, we also require some attempt at explanation for events; things must not 'just happen' all the time. Thus the hero of *The King of the Golden Mountain* arranges that his father has become impoverished by the loss of his merchant ships. The necessity in which he is consequently placed does something to explain his listening to the preposterous suggestion of the dwarf. This explanation is not very convincing, however. The rationalizations of story rarely are, but the deep satisfaction which we obtain from stories makes us ready to be easily satisfied with any rationalizations which are offered.

Particular places are often chosen for the events of story, even though they all take place in the hero's mind. We could almost follow Sir Gawain's route to the Green Chapel on a map, noting where he is in relation to North Wales, Anglesey, Holyhead and the Wirral. Kings are given countries, such as Tristan's father's 'Parmenie' and King Mark's Cornwall. Just as stories are often set in identifiable places, so are their events usually given some point of time for their occurrence, or some duration of time. These times are of a vague and ritual nature; 'Christmas', 'New Year', 'fifteen days' and 'seven years' are references to time which are as common in romances as 'once upon a time' is in folktales. The purpose of these references to time and place is not only to give credibility to the pretence that the events of the story actually occurred historically, but also to distance the events of the story. They are set in exotic lands, so that their strangeness may be thus explained, and it need not be believed that they are happening at the actual time of the telling of the story. They are also set in times that we know, such as festivals, but in years long past, when such things might be believed to have occurred. The time of the happening of a story is any time but the present. These stratagems help to give aesthetic distance, so that we may pretend, if we wish to do so, that the story does not deeply concern us personally.

Let us now approach the forms which stories take from another angle to see what further light can be thrown on their morphology. Vladimir Propp, in his *Morphology of the Folktale*[1], has defined the motifs of story in terms of their function and finds that they can be quite precisely delineated. He is, of course, viewing the story from the outside. Propp was not concerned with meaning, but his unique analysis of form and function in story, directing one's attention away from the study of individual stories as documents, leads to further insights into the activity of story. In this book his work will not be referred to in such a way as to give the reader a full understanding of his particular approach and achievement; it will be referred to in relation to the insights to which his research has given rise.

Vladimir Propp first of all, notes that the initial situation involves some kind of 'lack'. The hero is enduring, or about to endure, some misfortune. He may be without something which he regards as essential for happiness, and there may well be a villain involved in this situation. The hero then leaves home, either voluntarily as a 'seeker hero' in quest of his fortune, or involuntarily as a 'victim hero'. In each case, he experiences an adventure, usually involving a villain, and he is often helped by a magically powerful 'donor', who will only help those who prove themselves to the donor as worthy of help. These experiences are, from first to last, tests of the hero's character. The donor may be an old woman or a dwarf whom the protagonist has helped, or a dead man who has reason to be grateful to him. He may be a prisoner whom the protagonist has released or a grateful beast. There then ensues some form of contest, usually taking the form of a battle with a villain, and the hero wins. Upon this event, the hero returns home. There may, upon his return, be renewed misfortune or villainy, in which case everything begins anew, with a renewed quest, a successfully completed ordeal, perhaps involving the magical help of a donor, and another return.

When the return takes place it may be in disguise; the hero's arrival may be unrecognized. There may then be some test in which the unrecognized hero proves triumphant and is consequently recognized. The recognition may be spontaneous, or it may be the result of the witnessing of the hero's triumph, and both kinds of recognition may be aided by some kind of mark, like a wound, or a possession, such as a ring. The false hero or villain is then exposed, and the hero is, in some way, given a new appearance. The villain is punished and the hero's triumph is often expressed in terms of marriage to a princess and the ascent to a throne. However, a new act of villainy may once again postpone the end. The apparent essential form of initial lack, leaving home, adventures, victory, return and recognition, may not be enacted once only. A new act of villainy brings about a repetition of this form. Within this framework are a variety of possible events, to which Vladimir Propp gives detailed attention. For the purpose of this study, it is enough to say that there may or may not be a donor and a villain; there may even be no actual departure from home, but there is always some misfortune, followed by a struggle which results in a victory for the protagonist. The consequence of this victory is recognition of the protagonist as triumphant and splendid.

Applying the findings of the present study to Propp's findings, the 'lack' is how the hero describes the state of his feelings at the beginning of his story. The initial situation is presented to us as one which is causing some dissatisfaction, and it is abandoned for a transference to a place of adventure, where the dissatisfaction can be resolved by the venting of the feelings present in the initial situation. In the place of adventure, deeper disguises may be used to make possible the full enactment of the protagonist's wishes. The 'lack' is a situation experienced in the inner world of the protagonist's mind, and so is the struggle, which is the conflict between his opposing feelings. The victory is also an essentially inner feeling. The acclaim of the world represents the fact that the hero now sees himself as he wishes to see himself.

Cat-Skin is, in the main, a victim heroine, while the hero of *The Golden Bird* is a seeker hero, and the hero of *The King of the Golden Mountain* is first a victim and then a seeker hero. Nevertheless, it can be seen that they are all really seeker heroes and heroines: however they may represent themselves, they wish to leave home and go to a place of adventure. They have arranged everything, including the villains and donors. Villains may well be themselves, like the ugly dwarf in *The King of the Golden Mountain*, and so may donors, like the fox in *The Golden Bird*.

In the place of adventure there is a situation parallel, in some way, to the initial situation. A story may have just one place of adventure, or, as in the case of *Tristan*, there may be many, the hero moving on from one to the next, re-enacting the preoccupations of the initial situation in each one, until he feels that he has achieved the triumph of his paramount wishes. Vladimir Propp calls the repetition of leaving home, adventure, victory and the return home to recognition, an entry into another 'move', and that term will be adopted here, although the repetition observed in this study is not the same as that which Propp was observing. While Propp's observed repetitions refer to cycles of events, those of this study refer to cycles of thought concerning the central feelings of the story. *Cat-Skin* is a story with two moves, the initial move and the place of adventure. *The King of the Golden Mountain* has three moves, the initial move and two adventure moves. *The Golden Bird* has four moves, the initial move, followed by a long and complex adventure move, and two moves concerned with resolution of guilt about the feelings in the story. It may be observed that moves tend to be divided off from one another by a journey taking the form of some kind of exile in a wilderness or on the sea. In some stories, such as that of *Tristan*, the protagonist's second move takes the form of a sojourn in a humble, loving home, which expresses another way in which he sees, and wishes to see, his initial situation.

Of the many multi-move stories, perhaps the best example for study is the medieval romance of *King Horn*.[2] The story is as follows. There is a kingdom called 'Sudene', an island where King Allof reigns with his queen. They have a son Horn. Of all his companions, Horn has a particular love for two: Athulf who is 'the best' and Fikenild who is 'the worst'.[3] King Allof is then killed by Saracen pirates, and Horn is set adrift with his two favourite companions, because the pirates are afraid that he will avenge his father. The boys land in a country called Westnesse and are received by King Aylmer. Horn's royal birth is not known, but Rymenild, the king's daugher, falls in love with him, and tells him that he may marry her. Horn protests that he is only of low birth, saying that it would be no fair wedding between a thrall and the king.[4] Rymenild faints at this response of his, but it is soon clear that Horn intends to accept the princess's love. She persuades her father to knight him, and Horn undertakes to prove himself before marrying Rymenild. He soon distinguishes himself by killing a band of Saracen pirates. Meanwhile, Rymenild dreams that a fish has broken her net, and Horn interprets the dream as meaning that some ill-wisher will destroy their happiness.[5] And, sure enough, Fikenild tells the king that Horn has seduced Rymenild and intends to destroy the king. The king believes Fikenild when he finds Horn and Rymenild in each other's arms. Horn is exiled and sets sail for Ireland.

In Ireland, he adopts the name of Godmod[6] (Goodmind) and serves as a knight under King Thurston. Here he avenges his father's death by killing an invading giant Saracen, who appears at Christmas and who, he knows, was the very man who killed his father.[7] He remains at Thurston's court for seven years, but refuses the hand of the princess in marriage, which is offered to him by the king.

Meanwhile, Rymenild is promised to King Mody of Reynis, and sends a messenger to find Horn, but, while he manages to deliver the message, he is drowned before he can bring Rymenild the news that Horn will return. Horn returns, disguised as a beggar, his neck blackened with coal-dust, and gets into the castle.[8] He makes himself known to Rymenild by making puns about drinking horns, by alluding to a fishing net which has been set for seven years, and by dropping into her cup a ring which she has given him. He finally wipes off the black disguise, as he asks her if she does not now recognize him. Then he kills the king to whom she is promised, and confronts her kingly father with his true identity and the assertion that he had been exiled because the king had believed the lies of Fikenild. Horn then announces that he is leaving the court to win back his heritage, and that he will return as a king to claim Rymenild as his queen. He sets off to do so, with his friend Athulf, and is successful in regaining his kingdom and restoring his mother. Meanwhile, however, Fikenild builds a castle and tries to force Rymenild into marrying him.[9] The king does not dare forbid him to do so. Horn has a warning dream, re-enters the castle disguised as a harper and kills Fikenild. He then rewards the faithful, and gives Athulf in marriage to King Thurston's daughter in Ireland. He and Rymenild rule in his kingdom of Sudene.

This romance is an admirable example of the story with a decided, clearly purposeful structure, giving expression to an apparently ludicrous subject-matter. Why is Horn in disguise at the courts of King Aylmer and King Thurston? There seem to be plenty of kings in the neighbourhood; why does he not enlist their help in regaining his kingdom? This would be in the interests of all the kings, if their kingdoms are going to be able to resist the onslaughts of lawless pirates. Then, as King of Sudene, Horn would hardly have been an unsuitable suitor for the hand of Rymenild. There is no conceivable reason why Horn should pretend to be a thrall, and if King Aylmer really thinks that he is one, why does he believe this low-born stranger to be a danger to himself? How does Fikenild succeed in building a castle and setting himself up before a cowed king as a suitor for Rymenild? But these questions can be seen to be as ridiculous as the story itself appears to be. Even as we ask them, it is clear that the highly formalized structure of the romance is deeply concerned with a decided logic of quite another kind, and it could hardly have come into being and been preserved if this were not the case. The pattern of repetition which characterizes the multi-move story, is perhaps more obvious in this story than in any other. The hero passes from scene to scene, crossing water in between each one and arriving in disguise. In each scene we find the hero with a woman and two or three male characters. Every scene is associated with the court of a king. Let us examine the story briefly, sufficiently to discern the moves.

There are six moves. The first is in Sudene, the second in Westnesse, the third in Ireland, the fourth back in Westnesse, the fifth in Sudene once more, and the last in Westnesse. The hero makes his way through these moves as if he were performing a ritual, enacting variations on the same theme, until his conflicting feelings have been given full play and a resolution has been achieved. In the first move, he is a prince, arranging that his father should be killed and he himself exiled. In the next move, he is a thrall at the court of another king, and loves the princess, who is seen as a woman of authority and beyond his reach. This love is seen not only as forbidden but also as a threat to the king. The hero arranges that his feelings should be made known to the king and that he should be exiled. Crossing water, and arriving in disguise in Ireland, he recreates his central preoccupation once again. This time he is called Goodmind (or Cutbeard in some versions of the story),[10] and the king has become King Thurston, who also has a daughter. Thus far it has become clear that the social position and the name which the hero adopts for each move profoundly expresses the mood of the move. The hero abandons the name Horn in the third move, and both 'Goodmind' and 'Cutbeard' express the opposite in their different ways. In this mood, the hero conceives of that aspect of himself which wishes his father dead as a powerful and terrifying giant (the Saracen) and he destroys it. Emerging triumphant, he then renounces the princess, who is actually offered to him, and serves the king for seven years. In the fourth move, the hero returns to Westnesse as a beggar, but he later makes himself known, and the scene appears differently from the way in which it appeared in the second move. King Aylmer is no longer strongly felt: the hero is no longer afraid of him, and is openly and unashamedly 'Horn'. Rymenild no longer appears forbidden. In the second move, Horn conceives of the fishing net as meaning that some ill-wisher will destroy the lovers' happiness, and, sure enough, Fikenild betrays them to the king. Now, the net, together with the other recognition tokens, are freely expressed sexual jokes. The rival king, moreover, is now a King Mody whom Horn eliminates.

He no longer has a feeling that he has a powerful rival. In his fifth move, Horn crosses water to Sudene as the rightful claimant to the throne and makes himself king, restoring his mother to her position. In the sixth move, he returns to Westnesse, as a harper, to confront Fikenild, who has become his rival for Rymenild and is seeking to take her by force from her cowed father. Fikenild is the character who reported Horn to King Aylmer as seducing Rymenild and intending to destroy the King. It seems that he represents the hero's still lurking feeling that marrying his princess and becoming a king is an underhand deed against a reigning king. This feeling must be finally vanquished before the hero can triumph. When this conflict is at last resolved, there is no need for yet another move: Horn's story comes to a natural end.

King Horn illustrates the multi-move story at its simplest, and this chapter will not be complete without a discussion of a more complex example of the phenomenon. *The Odyssey*[11] is an excellent example of the multi-move story at its most mature. Unfortunately, a detailed study of the entire story has proved to be too long and involved for a clear discussion of the nature of the moves, and thus it will be necessary to limit detailed attention to some parts only. It will also be necessary to mention some of the characteristics of the moves at the outset, in order to give clarity to the discussion.

While *The Odyssey* takes the form of a series of moves, these moves are not distinguished by the arrivals and adventures of a single acknowledged hero: they are distinguished by changes of mood and consequent alterations in approach to the hero's preoccupations. He may never arrive at all in any acknowledged form; every one of the reflections in a move may be presented as those of others. Moreover, the reflections may be presented entirely in the form of conversation, rather than action. These conversations recall spectacular adventures, however, adventures which would have been well-known to Homer's audiences.

Entering the story as the hero, we go through it thought by thought, no matter how these thoughts are presented, and it becomes possible to see that, from the very beginning, the thoughts are closely linked; that certain precise thoughts are being expressed in a precise manner, in spite of the apparently profuse nature of the story. The hero (Homer and ourselves, joined with Odysseus) first thinks of the sacking of Troy: this involves thinking of Helen of Troy, Menelaus and Paris, and the restoration of Helen to her husband, mainly as a result of the skill of the hero. Then he thinks of the defiant act on the part of his companions against the sun god. Next he thinks of himself in the power of Calypso and Poseidon, whose magic powers are united in concentrating upon preventing him from returning home. One is motivated by love and the other by revenge. Clytaemnestra, Agamemnon and Aegisthus are next in his thoughts, together with the revenge of Orestes. Athene is visualized as supporting the hero's wishes to leave Calypso, and as not associating him with Aegisthus, the subject of the gods' angry thoughts, while, at the same time, blaming the gods for his frustration. She points out the sacrifices made by the hero on their behalf. Their revenge against the hero for his blinding of Polyphemus comes next in his thoughts, but the vengeful feelings are proclaimed as those of Poseidon alone, while the rest of the gods will help him. Zeus has been contemplated as the enemy of the hero but is now declared to be on his side.

Then the hero thinks of his home situation. It is significant that he does not do this until he has thought about the affairs associated with Helen and Clytaemnestra, and has also contemplated himself in relation to the gods. He has also first clinched his initial preoccupation in a vivid series of images. He is in the power of a beautiful witch, while a vengeful god lurks because of his blinding of this god's son. When he thinks of his home, the scene essentially contains a woman and a kingdom, both of which are desired ignominiously by young men, while the rightful owner lurks. This time the hero's position has shifted: he sees himself as the lurking, vengeful power. However, in this central scene of the story, it can be seen that the hero also appears as the son Telemachus and as the suitors. Following upon the hero's previous thoughts, we naturally step into the mind of Telemachus as he enters the story, and into the minds of the suitors. Thoughts of Paris and Odysseus, Aegisthus and Orestes have brought us naturally to this point: the hero as younger man is split into two—into a loyal son and into a usurper. Meanwhile, the hero also appears as the ruler and father, the rightful occupant of his position. He is contemplating the situation from three angles.

As Telemachus, the hero visits Nestor and finds favour with this old friend of Odysseus whom the gods have favoured. Nestor tells Telemachus that he is like his father and must also be like Orestes. He also tells the story of Aegisthus and Clytaemnestra, and urges Telemachus to visit Menelaus and Helen.

When the hero visualizes a visit to Menelaus and Helen, he sees them celebrating the wedding feasts of their daughter and of Menelaus' son. Upon the hero's arrival, they all grieve over the fates of so many who fought at Troy, and Helen drugs them to make them festive. Then they reminisce. Helen remembers Odysseus' entry into Troy as a beggar, and their consequent meeting there. Menelaus then recalls the entry into Troy in the Wooden Horse and also his adventure on the island of Pharos, when the shape-shifting Old Man of the Sea told him that sacrifice to Zeus and the other gods was essential before he, Menelaus, could get home. When Telemachus leaves Menelaus, the king gives him a bowl made of silver and gold, his most precious treasure.

The hero then thinks of the suitors' plan to waylay and kill Telemachus.

The moves do not take the form of celebrations of isolated feelings; mixed feelings are present in every one. Odysseus enjoys the voluptuous love of Calypso, but also longs to get away from her. He contemplates the idea of being both Aegisthus and Orestes as Zeus and Athene argue, and then, as he thinks of his preoccupations within the setting of his own home, he is Aegisthus, Orestes and a more fortunate Agamemnon. Next, he thinks of himself as a potential Orestes with a loving father (Nestor), but even here he has Nestor suggest a visit to Menelaus and Helen. His next thoughts are both voluptuous and sad. He enters Troy twice in disguise, once to meet Helen secretly and then to restore her to her husband. The scene is saddened by thoughts of frightening and vengeful fathers and the hero's need to make sacrifices for them if he is to return home. His mood then changes again, with his Aegisthus feelings coming uppermost, but he is in terror of these.

When one follows the story thought by thought one finds that these thoughts are expressed by a variety of characters, and there is nothing confusing about this, for the characters can all be seen to represent the hero and a very few other people about whom he is thinking. This is why we feel no bewilderment if we simply enjoy the story without seeking to analyse its structure. Such an analysis can cause confusion, unless we can make contact with our unconscious experience of the story.

While the move patterns just described characterize much of *The Odyssey*, other interesting patterns are discernable. A distinct series of moves are those which occur in Odysseus' own account of his adventures to the Phaeacians.

Here the story assumes the form of a vivid series of moves, the hero passing from one to the next across water and arriving in the acknowledged form of Odysseus, and in the unacknowledged form of his companions. The expression of conflicts is thus more clearcut.

Odysseus begins by praising his home from which the witches Calypso and Circe have tried to keep him. He says parents are held sweetest, even when the hero is far away. Then he tells of the sacking of Ismarus and theft of the wives: this is the first adventure after the sack of Troy, when the hero restored Helen to her husband Menelaus. A gale sent by Zeus follows the sack of Ismarus and then comes the adventure with the Lotus-Eaters, when many of the companions would have forgotten their home, had it not been for Odysseus. The adventure with Polyphemus comes next: he eats many of the companions but the hero succeeds in blinding him and tricking him, as 'Nobody'. The following move is the adventure with Circe, the witch who robs men of their manhood. Many of the companions become pigs when they encounter her, but Odysseus has an antidote against her powers which has been given him by the lovely god Hermes, who also advises him to charge the goddess with a sword and make her swear not to trick him. The hero triumphs as the lover of Circe, and then visualizes her as sending him and his remaining companions to the Underworld to propitiate the dead and gain the advice of Teiresias as to how to get home. The move in the lugubrious Underworld is one of conversation. Teiresias warns Odysseus about the cattle of the sun-god and about the situation at his home. He tells him that after defeating the suitors, he must set out again until he meets up with people who have never seen an oar, and there make a sacrifice to Poseidon. Thus the hero reflects on how his story will end. Then he encounters his mother and finds that he cannot embrace her ghost. After his mother, he sees many famous women, including Oedipus' mother, and then he has a feeling that he does not wish to continue with these reflections. We return briefly to an awareness that we are at the Phaeacians' feast, where the audience persuades the hero to resume his story.

The story is resumed, still in the Underworld. Odysseus says that he will tell how his companions lost their lives after the perils of the Trojan war, which had all been due to the whim of one unfaithful wife. Then he arranges that Persephone drives off all the women's ghosts, and men become the subject of his reflections. Agamemnon is conjured up, in sorrow, together with all who died owing to Aegisthus' ambition. Agamemnon tells his story, and warns Odysseus to arrive home in disguise, never trusting his wife, not even the faithful Penelope. Women are never to be trusted. The hero then conjures up Achilles, who is full of thoughts of his son and desires news of him. Odysseus tells him of his son's heroism at Troy and Achilles is filled with pride. Images of great men and tortured men follow, until Herakles appears saying 'Unhappy man. So you too are working out some such miserable doom as I was slave to when the sun shone over my head'.[12] The Underworld appears as a place of sorrow and unending despair, and the cries of myriad dead terrify the hero. Then he is suddenly filled with an overwhelming fear that dread Persephone might send him up from Hades' Halls some ghostly monster like the Gorgon's head. Upon this thought he leaves the Underworld at once.

The hero has experienced nightmare in this move and it is when he is thinking of women that his terror compels him twice to break off. He has tried to allay his terror over the thoughts which are gripping his mind. He has laid plans for the future of his story, viewing his conflicts as a son, when with Teiresias, and as a wronged husband, through Agamemnon. Through Achilles he thinks of a situation where a father is proud of a son who sacks Troy. This is viewed from the point of view of the son and the father. These efforts do not succeed: the move is pervaded by visions of heroic manhood brought low, and sinister women who offer horror and not love. As Helen destroyed men, so all women seem to do.

Helen's desirability led to the destruction of both sons and husbands. At the beginning of the story which he tells the Phaeacians, the hero echoes other thoughts which he has had of her, when he sacks Ismarus and steals wives. Next follow thoughts of a vengeful Zeus, and then comes a move which declares a longing to give up all thoughts of home. The hero desires a 'forgetting' process where his home is concerned, before he plunges into two moves in which he overcomes and mutilates a giant, and then overcomes and sleeps with a witch. The identity of the giant and the witch must not be known, but the hero does know it somewhere in his mind, as the nightmare in the dark Underworld reveals. The denial and repression declared in the scene with the Lotus Eaters, where the hero denies his forgetting, is not wholly effective. He is horror-stricken by what he does to the giant and the witch and, at the same time, by what they might do to him.

The imagery in *The Odyssey* will be considered in detail in the next chapter. Here the purpose is to observe how the hero gives form to his thoughts, and it can now be seen that, in his story told to the Phaeacians, he is splitting up his emotional experience and expressing isolated aspects of it in separate moves. Each move is closely linked to those before and after it, and the order given to the moves is deeply important.

When Odysseus escapes from the Underworld, he returns to Circe and tells her his experience there. She then gives him a full account of his future adventures, describing many horrors which Teiresias did not mention: the Sirens, the Wandering Rocks, and Scylla and Charybdis. Immediately these adventures begin. The hero encounters the Sirens, Scylla and Charybdis and the cattle of the Sun-god and in each adventure he divides his experience into that of Odysseus and that of his companions. The imagery will not be dwelt upon here, but it can clearly be seen that the first two adventures express feelings which the hero has about women, while the third expresses defiance against a god. After this defiance comes Zeus' hurricane in which the remaining companions all perish. Odysseus, lashed to a mast and keel, is washed back to Charybdis, who sucks down the mast and keel, while the hero clings to her fig tree until she should return them. When she does so, he escapes and is washed to the island of Calypso.

Here his story told to the Phaeacians ends. The events between the last conversation with Circe and the arrival on the island of Calypso are so closely linked that they might be regarded as one move containing within it a series of moves which are too closely linked to be separated from each other. Such a structure also exists in the second moves of *Cat-Skin* and *The Golden Bird*, but in these folktales there is a repetition not only of mood but also of action, which the moves between Circe and Calypso do not show. The emotional experience of Odysseus, in his story, is split up, so that the moves contrast with each other, but they are also bound together by being presented first in Circe's warning. They end, moreover, with the hero's return to Charybdis and then his final landing on the island of yet another witch. The whole effect is of a sequence of images exploring the hero's feelings about women with fear and fascination. These feelings create the unforgettable witches Circe, the Sirens, Scylla, Charybdis, and Calypso, the first and the last of whom are more fully dwelt upon, and emphasize the preoccupations of the whole sequence. The brief moves of the Sirens, and Scylla and Charybdis, express profoundly experienced fragments of feeling about woman, their voices and their devouring aspects emphasizing their close link with the images of Circe and Calypso. On the island of the sun-god, woman is viewed in yet another terrifying form: she belongs to someone else, a man with fearsome powers.

Also apparent in *The Odyssey* is another, more familiar, kind of move, where the hero arrives unknown at the court of a king, and acts out his feelings. It is thus that Odysseus arrives at the Phaeacian kingdom of King Alcinous and Queen Arete, where he meets their daughter Nausicaa, and comes to tell the story of his adventures hitherto. However, the chief arrival in the whole story is the last one, where Odysseus arrives in disguise in his own kingdom of Ithaca. It is during this last long move that Odysseus gives full play to all his feelings, and achieves a resolution of his conflicts.

It might now be observed that, in a sense, the hero has been concerned up to this point with his initial situation. It has been explored from every possible angle in the form of a wandering journey of the spirit, during which the prevailing feeling is a desire to return home. As this desire overcomes all others at last, the hero crosses water and arrives in disguise at his home.

The hero's full expression of feeling cannot be described in detail here; there is space only to examine the general structure given to the events in this place of adventure. The hero is disguised as an aged beggar, and he arrives first at the home of Eumeus the swine-herd and then at the royal court. He is full of lying tales about himself, every detail of which is significant. He is playing with ideas of being all kinds of men with varying origins, but there is also an obsession with Idomeneus who is mentioned in all of the lying tales. Homer would have assumed our knowledge of this character: he does not directly mention that Idomeneus was famous as the Cretan leader at Troy who was caught in a storm on his way home and who vowed to sacrifice the first thing that met him, if he returned safe. This proved to be his own son.[13] As the hero tells his lying tales, in one of which he says he has killed Idomeneus' son, the suitors are still lying in wait to ambush Telemachus.

Telemachus leaves Menelaus and Helen, avoids Nestor and picks up a fugitive seer, Theoclymenus, who has killed a kinsman and who is descended from Melampus, who secured a princess from a king and gave her to his brother. Meanwhile, Odysseus talks to Eumeus, with whom he is staying, and learns that he was a king's son made slave by the perfidy of his nurse, who had been led astray by the love-making of one of the pirates. He then grew up in the care of Odysseus' parents until there was a danger of his becoming too attached to their daughter. Eumeus then tells Odysseus about the grief of the hero's parents at his loss; his mother has died, pining for him.

Telemachus returns safely, and there is a loving meeting between him and Odysseus in Eumeus' hut. They lay plans for Odysseus' return to his rights.

Odysseus then moves from the swineherd's hut to the palace. Here he continues to play the role of a beggar, while the suitors and others insult him. He encounters the beggar, Irus, who sneers at him until he defeats and ejects him, telling him to stop playing the part of a beggar-king. The suitors determine to send Irus to King Echetus the Ogre, who will cut off his nose and ears, and castrate him. Meanwhile, Odysseus, the one who is really playing the rôle of beggar-king, continues to do so, having pin-pointed the fact that he is doing so and cancelled it out in his mind through the scapegoat, Irus. He has alluring visions of Penelope which he acknowledges through the feelings assigned to the suitors. She is beautiful, faithful to her husband, and distressed at the shameful treatment of the beggar (Odysseus). When she talks to Telemachus about the treat-ment of the beggar, he apologizes, saying that he does not have full powers over the suitors, but that he knows right from wrong, no longer being a child.

Another particularly significant event during this part of the hero's story is his nurse's recognition of him. She had mothered him and when she now baths him, she recognizes the scar from a wound on his thigh, which he received from a boar when visiting his grandfather in his youth. It was this grandfather, a liar and a thief, who had suggested that his name should be Odysseus, meaning 'the victim of enmity'.

Odysseus lies about his identity to Penelope but lets her know that Odysseus' arrival is imminent. She is constantly visualized as mourning for the hero, and as beautiful like a goddess. One of the maid-servants jeers at the beggar-hero for ogling at the women. He sleeps on the floor while the women and suitors make love, and the love-making angers him. Athene asks him why he is unhappy in his own home.

Telemachus is meanwhile maintaining that he cannot force his mother to marry again; he can only advise her that it would be wisest. The suitors are plotting his death, and Athene prolongs events so that Odysseus may feel his anguish deeply.

Thus the hero's feelings war with each other at length, the hero savouring them to the full as he contemplates Penelope. The jeering suitors fling insults and a cow's hoof at him, but he is not a beggar; he is a hero hiding his splendour. At last, Penelope confronts the suitors with Odysseus' bow and arrows for the contest which she has devised for her hand. The beggar-hero asks to try the bow and he is threatened by the suitors with the punishment suffered by the drunken Centaur at King Peirithous' house, who had his ears and nose cut off. They threaten Odysseus with the punishment of Echetus the Ogre. Penelope intervenes, saying that Odysseus is not a suitor: he has not thought of such a thing.

Next follows the battle in the hall, when the hero declares himself. Athene helps, reminding Odysseus of his courage when he fought the Trojans for the white arms of high-born Helen.

All is triumph over the suitors and following this comes the recognition scene with Penelope, who tests him as to his knowledge of the nature of their bed, which has a living trunk as a bedpost. Then they make love, but just before they do so, Odysseus tells Penelope that he will have to leave her again on the journey to find people who have never seen an oar.

After the love-making, the hero thinks of the suitors' encounter with Agamemnon in the Underworld, and contemplates the different points of view both parties entertain where the events which have taken place are concerned.

Next the hero sees himself as reunited with his father, Laertes, bringing a joy to the grieved old man which greatly improves his appearance. Then he has Zeus tell his daughter Athene that it has been her idea that Odysseus should return and avenge himself on his enemies. She must act as she pleases but Zeus thinks that Odysseus should now be king and the rest should be forgotten.

A battle in Ithaca follows, but after the hero's father kills the chief suitor's father, Athene calls an end to the fighting. The intervention of Zeus and Athene, in her familiar disguise as Mentor, stops Odysseus' revenge and, for fear of offending ever-watchful Zeus, Odysseus settles for peace. Thus his story ends.

The scenes in Ithaca all make up one long and very detailed move, in which the hero explores all his feelings in relation to his having placed himself at the court, near the Queen. He sees himself as the King, rightfully there, but also plays with the idea that he is the reverse, in his beggar form. Furthermore, he plays with the idea that he is a loyal son to the King, while also giving full play to thoughts of himself as a mere usurper. He finally overcomes all that the suitors represent in him and is then united with the Queen as her husband. However, he still feels that he must propitiate Poseidon, in a place where no one recognizes an oar, and he still has a need to make his peace with the two other father-figures, Laertes and Zeus. When such reconciliations are spoken of or achieved, the hero's conflicts are at an end and his story is done.

NOTES TO CHAPTER 5

1. Vladimir Propp, 'Morphology of the Folktale', in *The International Journal of American Linguistics*, Vol. 24, No. 4 (October 1958).

2. *King Horn*, edited by Joseph Hall (Oxford, 1901). The summary in this book has been made from the London text.

3. *Ibid.*, London text, ll. 26–30.

4. *Ibid.*, ll. 427–8.

5. *Ibid.*, ll. 656–86.

6. *Ibid.*, l. 773.

7. *Ibid.*, ll. 875–81.

8. *Ibid.*, ll. 1069–1162.

9. *Ibid.*, ll. 1403–20.

10. In the Oxford text, Horn takes the name Cubert; in the Cambridge text, Cutberd; in *Horn et Rimenild*, Gudmod; and in *Horn Childe and Maiden Rimnild*, Godebounde. In the simplified ballad versions, known as 'Hind Horn', the hero does not give himself a new name, but he experiences the seven years' exile over the sea, the dramatic significance of which is his separation from the princess and her angry father. A study of the many versions of the Horn story, giving detailed consideration to all their differences of expression, in order to investigate the extent to which the story has remained unchanged or become altered during transmission, would be fruitful.

Varying versions of *Hind Horn* may be found in the following publications: F. C. Child, *English and Scottish Popular Ballads*, edited by H. C. Sargent and G. L. Kittredge (London, 1904), No. 17, p. 31; *The Oxford Book of Ballads*, edited by Arthur Quiller-Couch (Oxford, 1920), No. 33, p. 142; *The Oxford Book of Ballads*, edited by James Kinsley (Oxford, 1969), No. 32, p. 112; *The Book of Narrative Poetry*, compiled by John R. Crossland (Glasgow, 1937), p. 45.

11. *Homer: The Odyssey*, translated by E. V. Rieu (Penguin Books, 1946).

12. *Ibid.*, p. 188.

13. H. J. Rose, *A Handbook of Greek Mythology* (London, 1928), p. 291.

6 *Imagery*

STORIES HAVE BEEN emerging as essentially pictorial by nature, like dreams. The language of imagery is far more difficult to interpret than that of words, and, ideally, a study of story would leave the actual process of interpretation to the individual insights of every reader. He should simply be led inside the story and left there, the natural process which takes place when he is listening, but if there is to be a study of the characteristics of story as an art form, it is unfortunately necessary for this book to present the reader with some interpretation as working material for the study. The reader will often disagree, and have other insights, but it is hoped that, far from finding this an unpleasant experience, he will find it exciting. This chapter on the most striking features of imagery makes no more claim than that it might be a spring board for further discovery.

Several striking features of imagery have already emerged. The most important is that, while it is a language, the significance which it is expressing is much less fixed than it is in the case of words. There could not be a dictionary for imagery, even though there are certain images which tend to be used to express particular meanings. A study of these particular images may lead to a belief that the use of analogy would be helpful: one is tempted to assume that if a symbol conveys a certain meaning in one case, it must have the same meaning in another. This study has revealed that this would be far more misleading than helpful. It is becoming clear that every image must be contemplated within the context of the dream or story to which it belongs, and that that context should be viewed from a position in the mind of the hero. One is on safest ground if one approaches each image in a story as a new creation on the part of the hero; however well-known it might be to us, it has been arbitrarily chosen by him to express his own feelings. It is wisest to assume that when he conjures up an image, he is not interested in how else it may have been employed by other people. When he creates a story, just as when he creates a dream, his whole concern is with his own urgent feelings.

This imposes an important limitation on this study. Each image requires an individual approach, as, at the same time, it is studied in the entire pictorial sequence in which it appears. One must enter each story, forgetting all others, and ponder on every detail of it. The task is made still more difficult by the fact that an image is capable of more than one interpretation and there will always be meaning which is eluding the researcher. As has already been observed in the limited studies in this book, the chained men and Tristan's dragon have multiple significance owing to multiple preoccupations in the protagonist's mind. The many meanings expressed by a single image may oppose each other, so that the image is, strictly speaking, a paradox, but this does not disturb the audience of a story, as it enjoys an image. The audience may select one meaning, or it may appreciate, unconsciously, the reality of the presence of them all.

There is a distinction between symbols and the rest of the imagery of story. A symbol is a picture of something which we know in the external world, but which we are picturing in order to give expression to an inner experience. In everyday life we may not see a connection between the object pictured and the feelings which we have expressed through conjuring up a picture of it in a dream or a story. There is a tendency to understand the symbol at its face value. A beast of prey may always be assumed to represent a beast of prey, and while it might indeed do so, it might equally represent human feelings which are deemed to be savage in some way. Lions, tigers, wolves and other such animals are, in fact, frequently employed as symbols of the more violent human feelings, in dreams and in literature, and to take such a symbol at its face value is to ignore the likelihood that it is a symbol. The context of the dream or story will help us to decide whether the beast is intended to be simply an animal or whether it is intended as a symbol. A symbol is a substitute for that which we really mean. It is essentially something representing something else or several other things, and it is chosen with intention, to express emotional experience which is felt to be important. If the beast of prey is a symbol, it may represent any of a great number of human experiences, and it may represent many at once. It might, for instance, represent both aggression and dignified nobility. Whatever the beast represents, it will have been chosen precisely because the dreamer or story-teller feels at any given moment that it will express that which he is seeking to express.

There is also a process whereby we create pictures of things which are not known in the actual world. This study has already met with witches such as Scylla, and with Tristan's dragon and the golden bird. While these images are apparently crazy, they are also familiar, this familiarity being too deep to be explained away by their place in tradition. We know all about them somewhere in our minds. The difference between such images as these and symbols is that the former are obviously related to our feelings, while the latter can pose as representing no more than objects. In stories, apparently crazy images join together with symbols in a pictorial sequence to express the hero's feelings. During the contemplation of a complex image, such as Scylla, it is important to study every detail.

Images represent only that which the protagonist wishes them to represent at any given moment of his story. By entering into Tristan's mind, we experience with him his sensations of growing larger and smaller as his feelings about himself alter, becoming a monstrous giant or a shrivelled dwarf. The scene in which 'Dwarf Tristan'[1] appears exemplifies the subtle ability of imagery to give expression to multiple moods and intentions, producing, as it does so, an atmosphere combining humour and sadness.

The name 'Dwarf Tristan' draws attention to the frequent importance of names in story. Names often express how the hero is seeing himself and others in his story. He may choose already famous names, like 'Sir Gawain' and 'Morgan the Fay', with meaningful intent; or, with equally decided purpose, prefer a simple description like 'king', 'shepherd', or 'gardener's son'. Many actual names in story bear particular significance. 'Tristan' itself is an example, and so are such names as Rivalin, Blancheflor, Cat-Skin and Allerleirauh. Of all stories perhaps *The Odyssey* is the most tantalizing where names are concerned: as in the case of many western European stories, the changes of time have added to the obscurity of many of them. Even where significance may be discerned, it is often ambiguous.[2] In *King Horn* is exemplified the great importance which names may bear: the hero changes his name during the course of his story to express changes of feeling, and while these names may vary in different versions, they express the same feelings.

As soon as one embarks on the study of an image in its context, one can see why no image in a story can effectively be studied in isolation from the rest of the story's pictorial sequence. Each image is but an element in the expression of the whole meaning of the story.

Let us consider the image of Scylla in its context. Scylla is on the higher of two rocks, which rears its peak up into black cloud. The rock cannot be climbed by man, and half-way up it there is a misty cavern, unreachable by any arrow shot from a ship below. In the cavern lives Scylla, 'the creature with the dreadful bark', which is no louder than a new born pup's. She is a 'horrible monster' with

> twelve feet, all dangling in the air, and six long necks, each ending in a grisly head with triple rows of teeth, set thick and close, and darkly menacing death. Up to her middle she is sunk in the depths of the cave, but her heads protrude from the fearful abyss, and thus she fishes from her own abode, scouting

around the rock for any dolphin or swordfish she may catch, or any of the larger monsters which in their thousands find their living in the roaring seas. No crew can boast that they ever sailed their ship past Scylla without loss, since from every passing vessel she snatches a man with each of her heads and so bears off her prey.[3]

This image is most immediately linked with that of Charybdis, which is on the lower rock. The distance between the two rocks is

no more than a bowshot. A great fig-tree with luxuriant foliage grows upon the crag, and it is below this that dread Charybdis sucks the dark waters down. Three times a day she spews them up, and three times she swallows them down once more in a horrible way.[4]

The hero first has Circe warn him about Scylla and Charybdis and then, after leaving her, he experiences them. Before this, he experiences the Sirens, whose singing bewitches all men, drawing them to them, where they meet only with death. The companions are protected from this fate by having their ears plugged, and Odysseus is protected by being bound to the mast. Thus he hears the luring voices, but cannot be lured. Nevertheless, his next thoughts are significantly of Scylla and Charybdis, and the devouring of many of his men.

Before the images of the Sirens, and Scylla, and Charybdis, comes the sequence beginning with Odysseus' leaving Troy for home. This is presented as the beginning of his story for the Phaeacians. When Troy is finally entered, Helen is restored to her husband. Here one has to banish all thoughts of history, and seek to grasp consciously the part which is being played by references to Troy in the sequence of images which is the story of *The Odyssey*. As a reaction to the outcome of the siege of Troy, the hero's first adventure upon leaving for home is to sack Ismarus, kill its defenders and take its wives. A large number of the companions are lost in this adventure, and a gale from Zeus follows, which all the company survive. Next, the hero thinks of the Lotus-eaters, where he may forget the home for which he expressed love at the beginning of this sequence. He represents himself as resisting the desire, and then thinks of an adventure with an ogre, Polyphemus.

Polyphemus is a one-eyed ogre who is shepherd to his great flock of sheep. When the company reach his home in a cave, he is not there, and there are thoughts of stealing some of the cheeses and young animals. Odysseus, however, wishes to see the ogre and hopes to receive some friendly gifts from him. While waiting for him, the company eats one of his beasts. On arrival, Polyphemus drives his milking ewes into the cave, leaving the male animals outside. The company is already in the cave, having been waiting there, and the ogre closes the entrance with a huge stone. Having milked his ewes and lit a fire, the ogre sees the company and hears their overtures for hospitality with a 'pitiless heart'. His response is to seize two of the companions, dash their brains out and devour them. This he does for several meals, keeping the company trapped in the cave. Then Odysseus makes him drunk with wine and tells him that his name is 'Nobody'. While the ogre lies in a drunken sleep, the company bores his eye out with a fire-hot olive stake. As Polyphemus yells and people come to find out what the trouble is, he calls out that it is 'Nobody's treachery, no violence, that is doing me to death'. Thus he receives no help. The company are still faced with the problem as to how they are to escape from the cave, for, by means of feeling, the blinded ogre seeks to prevent them from doing so. However, Odysseus hits on the idea that they should escape by hanging underneath the bodies of the sheep, whose top-sides the ogre feels as they pass out of the cave. Odysseus selects the finest of the rams to carry him after he has lashed his companions to other rams, with a ram on each side of them to protect them. Polyphemus wonders that the huge ram is lagging behind and asks him if he is grieving for his master's eye. The company escape, taking the sheep with them, and Odysseus then taunts the ogre from a distance. The angry Cyclops hurls a huge rock at them as they are putting out to sea and, against his companions' judgement, Odysseus then reveals his identity to him. Polyphemus says that it was foretold that a man called Odysseus would rob him of his sight, but he was expecting this man to be splendid in size and strength, not 'a puny, good for nothing little runt'. He thinks Poseidon will restore his sight for him since he is his father, but Odysseus says he would not do so and he shouts his wish that he could rob Polyphemus of life and send him to Hell. The ogre then prays to Poseidon that the god might prevent him from reaching his home. If he should reach home, let him do so 'in evil plight', late and with all his companions dead. When he lands 'by a foreign ship, let him find trouble in his home'.[5] Polyphemus then hurls a vast boulder at the ship and misses the end of the steering oar by inches. All that remains of the company then feast on the stolen sheep.

In this deeply complex move, the hero visualizes himself as entering the cave home of an ogre with a single eye. He wishes to rob the ogre and yet also to receive his hospitality. He has summoned up a vision of a man who is gigantic, ferocious and beyond all law, and wishes to encounter this man. Upon doing so he enjoys being a little trickster, investing his monster with both stupidity and crudity. He makes it appear that Polyphemus is the villain: every-

76

thing in this move is made to appear as the hero wishes it to appear. The whole scene needs to be dwelt on imaginatively from this point of view. One must visualize such details as that of the ogre milking ewes in his cave home, which the hero has invaded, and then the act of mutilation and the hero's subsequent riding out of the cave under the ogre's finest ram. The hero attributes to this adventure the enmity of Poseidon and the trouble at his home.

The logic of this is equalled by that to be found in the transition from thoughts of Polyphemus to thoughts of Circe. Circe is a beautiful witch who gives men food which robs them of their manhood, turning them into pigs. The hero can counteract her power by possessing a herb with a black root and a milk-white flower, which is given to him by Hermes, 'looking like a young man at that most charming age when the beard first starts to grow'.[6] Then, when Circe has fed him and subsequently struck him with her wand, the hero must draw his sword and rush at her. In terror the witch will then invite him to her bed. Even then, she must give the hero a solemn oath that she will not be up to any more of her tricks, or when she has the hero stripped she may rob him of his courage and manhood.

Some of the hero's fears of women seem to be expressed here, and in this move he sees himself triumphantly overcome them. A beautiful young god, expressing the way in which he wishes to see himself, gives him, as an antidote to the woman's power to unman him, a herb with a milk-white flower and a black root. This significantly coloured plant expresses feelings which the hero has about the anatomy of woman, and picturing his feelings thus is a vital help to him. The milk-white flower above and the black root below, which is normally hidden and hard for a mere man to dig up, are essentially linked. The woman with milk is thought of also as black in that part which the hero feels he should not think of. His thoughts of her as a mother inhibit his desire for her, because of his fear of incest, but he counteracts this fear by putting himself in possession of the whole plant and thus, he feels, of woman too. His fears create the image of the plant, but so also does his realization that woman is as natural as the plant. Looking at the plant and possessing it, beauty, milk and root, he is able to take food from Circe and then possess her sexually. He becomes the master with his sword, and with the reassurance given by the magic words of her oath.

The move of Circe is parallel to that of Polyphemus. First the hero is in the home of the ogre and then in that of the witch. The fact that Polyphemus and Circe are in their homes is vitally important, and it seems that the homes might really be the same home. The disguises are deep, but it is not surprising that the nightmare in the Underworld follows the adventures with the giant and the witch.

The final image in the Underworld is that of the Medusa's head, a culmination of the hero's thoughts about the people he meets in Hades, and his feelings about himself in relation to them. But the death pervading the move is also an essential part of the nightmare. Thoughts of death haunt every move of the hero's adventure: a part of himself dies in some of his companions, or death is imminent as a god rages. Just before the journey to the Underworld, a companion falls to his death from Circe's roof, and the hero encounters him in Hades before he sees anyone else. In Elpenor he sees himself in the land of the dead.

It is after he leaves the Underworld that the hero thinks of the Sirens, Scylla and Charybdis and the cattle of the Sun. Details often overtly link images, as does the idea of milk in Polyphemus' ewes and the herb of Hermes. Thus, in his thoughts of witches, the hero is haunted by voices. Circe has a 'woman's voice' and sings beautifully, the Sirens have musical voices with a fatal lure, Scylla has a 'dreadful' little yelp, and Calypso, last of all, has a 'woman's voice'. Odysseus thinks of the danger of being lured by women and both enjoys and overcomes this danger in his visions of Circe and the Sirens. Then, in Scylla and Charybdis, he has a nightmare vision of sexual experience with women. Woman's very sexuality is seen as devouring, and in some of his companions the hero experiences the devouring, while also avoiding it. Thoughts of devouring and of being devoured occur in several of the moves in this sequence. Polyphemus is seen as devouring, and, on the island of the Sun, it is the hero who, in his companions, does the devouring. He devours the cattle of the Sun, as he devours the sheep of Polyphemus, and the wrath which he feels must follow such thoughts drowns the companions whom he represents as performing this deed. The acknowledged hero, who did not, he tells us, devour the 'fine fatted cows'[7] of the Sun god, remains alone, to be swept back to the devouring Charybdis. Hanging on to her fig tree, he avoids being sucked down by her whirlpool, but she sucks down the mast and keel which he needs for survival on the stormy sea, and he can only escape when she spews them up again. When he does escape, he is washed to the island of Calypso, 'that formidable goddess with a woman's voice'[8] who loves him and wishes to hold him for ever on her island. He is fascinated by thoughts of love with her, but also wishes to escape from her power, which he sees as devouring in a spiritual sense. When, at last, he leaves the vaulted cave of the goddess, he faces another annihilating force: the rage of a god.

It has not been possible to give every detail here, though every detail is vitally important. However, as one considers the myriad details given in *The Odyssey*, one must not allow the end result of one's thinking to be fragmented. Just as our minds can see a meaningful picture, as we look at the thousands of brush strokes of an artist, so they can discern a meaningful picture, as they piece together all the minute elements of *The Odyssey*. Every element must be pictured in the mind. If one visualizes the mast and keel, for instance, in the context of the whole Charybdis scene, they might be revealed as linking together to form a symbol with vital meaning in the scene. Moreover, the vast number of characters in the story can be seen to express aspects of a very few people in the hero's mind, and the symbols and complex images also express these aspects and the hero's feelings about them. For example, aspects of woman appear to be expressed by the following: Athene, Helen of Troy, Clytaemnestra, Calypso, Circe, Penelope, the nurse Eurycleia, the impertinent maid-servant Melantho, Aphrodite, Nestor's daughter, Nausicaa, her wise mother Arete, Persephone, Odysseus' dead mother, all the famous dead women in their variety, the Gorgan Medusa, the Sirens, Scylla and Charybdis, the cattle of the Sun, Polyphemus' ewes, Phorcys' cove in Ithaca, Hermes' herb, Menelaus' bowl of silver and gold, the caves of Polyphemus and Calypso, and the city of Troy. Every character and every object has more than a superficial meaning: the bow and arrow of Odysseus, and the oar, which the hero must carry to a place where no one can recognize it, have deeper meanings than their obvious ones, and references to characters of myth and legend are deeply purposeful. Returning to the particular sequence of images which has just been studied, there must be an exploration of the rôle which the reference to the sack of Troy is playing in the sequence and, indeed, in the whole story. The reference will not be an idle one, and nor will the inclusion of Poseidon and Zeus in the story be merely conventional. Similarly, the fact that Nestor's palace actually existed must not divert attention from the rôle of the old king and his palace as images. They will have meaning for the hero in addition to their historical significance, which is one of their essential attributes in the story. The hero seizes upon historical characters and actual places as invaluable inclusions in the sequence of images which is united in the expression of inner feelings rather than historical actuality.

The hero's sacrifices to the gods must also be understood as meaning more to him than a mere rite. The hero is thinking in the language of fantasy, and the result of his ponderings is this series of images exploring his complex feelings in relation to a particular theme. As the hero thinks, the subjects of his thoughts are seen in varied and striking forms. Above all, the sequence of images associated with Scylla and Charybdis reveals our astonishing power to think about our mundane everyday emotional experience in a language of unforgettable grandeur, a language which combines forceful impact with the profoundly memorable.

As one approaches the imagery of story, one must not rationalize, and one must not judge it according to general interpretations exterior to the story. Troy and Zeus are images expressing profound feelings for the hero, like all the other images of the story, and their meanings depend upon their context. This context needs detailed study. An assumption, for instance, that the fox in *Sir Gawain and the Green Knight* represents, simply, cunning—even though he is described as 'wily' in the romance—will distort our whole understanding of the story. Let us examine the complex sequence of pictures representing Sir Gawain's thoughts in the castle near the Green Chapel,[9] visualizing each picture in its exact order. By doing this, this study hopes to demonstrate the difference between the results thus obtained and those obtained by study exterior to the story, introducing preconceptions and analogy.

The lord of the castle first sets out to hunt timorous deer, and selects the females, leaving the males. All this takes place on the edge of a forest, and there are a great number of does killed, pierced by arrows biting into their flesh. They have no chance against the hunters. Then the images depict the hero lying in bed and the lady creeping towards him. He feigns sleep and she sits on the side of his bed. The conversation is courtly but also direct on the lady's part, as she offers her body to the hero. The hero is all honour and chivalrously declines the offer. At the end of the witty dalliances, Gawain thinks of the stroke of an axe and it is then that the lady suggests a kiss. Gawain speaks as a knight, but he is lying in bed while a fully-dressed lady leans over him to kiss him, before departing. The rest of the day is spent gaily with the ladies, particularly with the beautiful young lady and the ugly old woman. The ugly old woman is included among those who give him delight. Upon this sequence of pictures succeed those of the lord beheading, cutting up and disembowelling his female deer. Their heads are cut off and parts of their bodies are devoured immediately by ravens and hounds. Then the hunters return to the roaring fires in the castle, and the lord hands the fine fat flesh of a doe to Gawain, while Gawain gives him a lady's kiss in return. There is a festive evening, and the next day the hunters set out in pursuit of an unnamed quarry. When they reach a quagmire, a ferocious boar leaps out at them from some bushes, and a fierce fight is underway. This fight is left while still in progress, as the images change to those of the hero in bed. The lady is by his side and a conversation about kissing begins. The lady tells Sir Gawain that he is strong enough to force her to give herself to him, if he so wishes. Gawain does not so wish, but he allows the lady two kisses, and after this private enjoyment, he enjoys the company of all the ladies again. Then the images return to the battle with the boar. Many people and hounds have been injured by the boar, but the beast is growing tired. It turns to rush into a hole by a running stream, and the lord comes up to it, as it stands with its back to the bank, scraping. It springs out at the lord and the battle ends in a near-by stream, where the lord at last kills the boar. Then he beheads it and cuts it up, before returning with the head borne in front of him. This head is given to Sir Gawain and Sir Gawain gives the lord the two kisses which he had received from the lady, in exchange. All is good humour again that evening and the bargain of the game is renewed. This time the hunt is a fox-hunt. The fox is wily, but finds himself in great danger, nevertheless, and, full of fear and woe, he rushes to the woods, pursued by threatening huntsmen shouting 'thief'. They often succeed in chasing him out into the open, but he cunningly wheels back into the woods again. As he leads them all a dance, the images change to a further sequence of pictures of Sir Gawain in bed. The lady comes to him again, and this time her breasts and back are bare. Sir Gawain's first thoughts are of his dread of the Green Knight, the axe and the Green Chapel, but the lady, laughing charmingly, swoops over him and kisses him. He gazes at her, and her attire, with rapture, and their conversation is full of joy and delight. There is an awareness of great peril between them, and the lady tempts the hero until he feels that he can scarcely resist. However, he does resist. He is asked if there is another woman in his life and he denies this, saying that he does not wish for there to be one as yet. The lady expresses her sorrow over this answer and kisses the hero again. She asks for the gift of a glove, and, upon Gawain's courteous refusal, offers him a gold ring. When this is refused, she offers him her green girdle, and this is refused, too, until the lady tells Gawain that it will protect him from death. Then, thinking of his danger at the Green Chapel, the hero accepts the girdle, promising, at the lady's request, to hide the transfer of its ownership from the lord's knowledge. After this, the lady kisses Sir Gawain again and leaves him. He rises, confesses his sins in a chapel and then makes merry among the ladies as if he has no care in the world. The images next return to the hunting field and the kill, which takes place just after the fox has rushed through a thicket. The lord is waiting for him there, outwitting him in doing so, and draws his sword. The fox swerves to avoid the sword and the hounds fall upon him. In no time he is reduced to a piece of skin. This skin is exchanged for the three kisses, but not for the green girdle, which Sir Gawain has hidden. The evening is represented as merry, but the hero has thoughts of the tryst at the Green Chapel and there is a woeful parting. The next images convey the bitter cold of a wintry dawn. There is a return to the wilderness.

It can be seen that these images represent a single sequence of feelings and that these feelings conflict with each other. There is excitement, terror, sexual desire, fear of mutilation and death, savagery and gentleness. Because the hero's feelings are complex and changeful, it is not possible to identify the hunter as the lord throughout the sequence, or the hunted as always being the hero: in part, the hero is the hunter, while thoughts of the lady are present in the hunted. Every detail of the descriptions of hunting and bedroom scenes builds up a consistent sequence of images expressing the hero's conflicting feelings about his desire for the lady. Some images, as in all stories and dreams, are better-defined and more striking than are others, and they are a key to the others during analysis. Particularly sharp are the images representing the exchanges, when the doe's flesh and the lady's kiss are seen together; when the boar's hewn-off head and the lady's two kisses are seen together; and when the fox's red skin is viewed, after the lady's three kisses are seen while her green girdle is hidden. The image of the boar is another vivid and less complicated picture. It represents the hero's vision of himself as he contemplates ravishing the lady and, consequently, confronting the lord.

No detail must be missed. Those such as thickets, holes, edges of woods and running streams are all important. But even as one does not miss a detail, and even as one comprehends some details more easily than others, one is faced with the task of grasping imaginatively the importance of each in relation to the others. A mistake here can result in distortion. The romance emphasizes that the fox is wily, so this is important. But the lord reduces the wily fox to a piece of skin and this is his gain at the end of the day. Sir Gawain's gain is a piece of silk, the green girdle. One is red, the other is green; one is shown, the other is hidden; one represents all that remains of a creature who tried to outwit the lord, and so what does the other represent? The answer can only be found as a result of a study of the whole romance, which will soon be made. The purpose now is to demonstrate how one must think. As one contemplates the cunning fox and Sir Gawain's feelings in the bedchamber, it is obvious that the fox's cunning, and his woe,[10] are not his only attributes. An important attribute is missing until we find it in the line: 'Then he was called thief and threatened often . . .'[11] The hunters do not shout threats at the fox because he is cunning but because he is a 'thief'. The hero is thinking about a fox hunt at this stage of his story because the fox is a thief and thus expresses feelings which he has about himself, while the successful hunt expresses his fears as to what may be the result of being a thief.

It appears from this investigation that the imagery of each story is a dynamic, living language[12] engaged in the expression of the story's particular themes. Its study essentially involves the meticulous study also of its context, and the taking of every precaution against introducing ideas which originate from outside the story.

NOTES TO CHAPTER 6

1. *Gottfried von Strassburg, Tristan*, translated by A. T. Hatto (Penguin Books), pp. 339–41.

2. This is a matter for Greek scholarship, but it is interesting for the layman to note the following possible meanings of names in *The Odyssey*: Eumeus: 'the well-disposed' (while the name Melanthius, given to the counterpart of Eumeus, is connected with 'black'); Medusa: 'she who rules'; Echetus: 'he who holds you fast'; Scylla: 'puppy'; Calypso: 'the hider'; Polyphemus; 'much spoken of', and the Sirens: probably connected with 'noose'. Homer tells us how Odysseus got his name (Book 19, 406–12)—from 'Odyssesthai', 'to be angry with'. In Book 19, 407, it seems to have the sense of 'being angry with', but elsewhere (Book 1, 62; 340; 423) it appears in a passive sense: 'victim of anger'; so also Book 19, 275. Penelope probably means 'a brightly plumaged duck' and Telemachus may be either 'he who fights from a distance' or 'he who is far from battle'. I am indebted to Mr Thomas Braun of Merton College, Oxford, for these and further illuminating comments on the names in *The Odyssey*.

3. *Homer: The Odyssey*, translated by E. V. Rieu (Penguin Books), p. 191.

4. *Ibid.*

5. *Ibid.*, pp. 153–4.

6. *Ibid.*, p. 163.

7. *Ibid.*, p. 198.

8. *Ibid.*, p. 201.

9. *Sir Gawain and the Green Knight*, edited by J. R. R. Tolkien and E. V. Gordon (Oxford, 1925), ll. 1126–1997.

10. *Ibid.*, l. 1717.

11. *Sir Gawain and the Green Knight*, translated by Brian Stone, p. 93.

12. For interesting studies in this field, see Roger Frétigny and André Virel, *L'Imagerie Mentale* (Geneva, 1968).

7   Transformation and Recognition

IN MANY TRADITIONAL stories, the difference between the beginning and the end appears to be no more than that the protagonist celebrates the victory of the feelings present in the initial situation. The feelings in such a story as *Cat-Skin* do not appear to undergo any fundamental change during the course of the story. This chapter will explore some stories in which the feelings in the initial situation do appear to undergo a crucial change, a factor which lies at the heart of the meaning of the story.

Among folktales, perhaps the best-known stories of this kind are those of *Beauty and the Beast* and *The Frog Prince*.[1] In these stories, the heroines' feelings about men, and consequently their images of them, become transformed, this transformation being the climax of the story. When the Frog Prince has been transformed into a handsome prince, at the end of the latter story, he tells the Princess that he had been enchanted by a malicious fairy, fated to remain in the form of a frog until a princess should take him out of the spring and let him sleep upon her bed for three nights. The Princess has broken this spell and he therefore wishes to marry her. The Prince's words that the Princess has broken the spell are perfectly true—but, since this is her story, it is also the Princess who cast the spell. Her attributing the enchantment to a malicious fairy expresses her apprehension of some of the feelings which led her to cast the spell. However, the important point to consider here is that the heroine's task is to break the spell which she has brought about. Only she can break it, freeing herself, essentially, from it.

There is a fundamental difference between the transformation scenes in *Beauty and the Beast* and *The Frog Prince* and that apparent in *Puss-in-Boots*. In the latter story, the hero, as the cat, turns the ogre into a mouse and eats it. His initial feelings have remained unchanged and he has merely attained his wish to feel splendid by diminishing the ogre and then absorbing all that he wanted of it into himself—at the same time annihilating it so that he can take over its status and possessions. Transformation scenes can, in fact, be seen to take two forms. The form apparent in *Puss-in-Boots* may also be discerned in *Alice in Wonderland* and *Through the Looking-*

Glass. While these latter stories are not traditional in origin and are therefore not strictly relevant, it is interesting to observe that they both end with Alice feeling bigger, while the Queen of Hearts has turned into cardboard and the Red Queen is shaken into a kitten.[2] Essentially, there has been no fundamental recognition in the heroine, leading her to change her images to others closer to reality: she merely attains a sense of her own splendour by diminishing those whom she apprehended as making her feel small. In the second form of transformation scene, that apparent in *Beauty and the Beast* and *The Frog Prince*, the heroine transforms her images as a result of having undergone a profound recognition of a reality, where she herself and others in her experience are concerned. It is this form of transformation scene which is apparent in the stories to be studied in this chapter.

The first story to be studied will be the medieval romance of *Libeaus Desconus*,[3] which is a multi-move story culminating in a transformation scene of particular interest.

The hero begins life in seclusion with his mother, and he is the bastard son of Sir Gawain. While hunting one day, he finds a dead knight, puts on his armour, and goes to King Arthur at Glastonbury to demand knighthood. As he does not know his own name, he is knighted as 'Libeaus Desconus', 'The Fair Unknown'. Gawain trains him, and he asks for the first adventure which may occur. This comes when Elene and her dwarf companion appeal to Arthur for a knight to deliver the imprisoned Lady of Sinadoune. They contemptuously accept 'The Fair Unknown' as their champion, and Elene jeers at him during their journey. Then she rides up to encounter Wylleam Celebronche,[4] still mocking the hero. Libeaus Desconus rides against this foe, who has attacked the 'Chappell Auntours' upon the 'Poynte Perylous', and, defeating him, dispatches him to King Arthur. Elene then apologizes to the hero. Next, Libeaus Desconus defeats and sends to King Arthur, three sons of a sister of Wylleam Celebronche, who try to avenge their uncle. In his third adventure, the hero rescues a maiden from two giants, one red and one black, whom he first finds by a fire.[5] He sends their heads to King Arthur, and when the girl is offered to him in marriage by her father, he declines her hand. This father, who is an earl, finds another way of rewarding him. The fourth adventure arises from Sir Giffroun's challenge to the world to bring forward a woman more beautiful than the lady whom he loves. If the person accepting the challenge fails, he must fight Sir Giffroun. The hero boldly brings Elene forward, but many people judge that the other lady is fairer. As a result, Libeaus Desconus challenges and defeats Sir Giffroun. There is a prize, a gerfalcon, which the hero sends to Arthur, and then he celebrates his victory with a feast.⁶ The dwarf has called the whole adventure dangerous, but the hero now passes on to a fifth adventure. He and his companions come across a hunt, and Elene likes the beautiful, many-coloured hound at the front of the pack so much that Libeaus Desconus catches it and gives it to her.⁷ Then the owner, Sir Otes de Lile, rides up and demands it back. The hero refuses and they fight. Sir Otes and twelve companions of his are defeated and are all dispatched to Arthur. The King now elects Libeaus Desconus to the Round Table.

After many more adventures which we are not told, Libeaus Desconus slays a huge, black giant who is besieging Dame d'Amore,⁸ the fair lady of the 'Yle d'Or'.⁹ But this lady uses magic powers to make the hero forget all his honour and his quest; he does nothing but enjoy her love, acting, at her request, as the lord of her city and castle. Dame d'Amore is described as an evil woman who knows sorcery. The hero looks into her face and thinks himself in paradise. After a year has passed, Elene appears and denounces him for neglecting his duties, making him feel deeply ashamed.¹⁰ He sets out once more on his quest, and, on the third day, he and his companions see the fair city of Sinadoune.¹¹ Accompanying himself, Elene and the dwarf, is Dame d'Amore's steward, acting as a squire. Reaching the castle the hero has to overcome Sir Lambard, the constable, in order to get in. Then the constable welcomes him saying that he must be Gawain's kin, but making the condition that he must fight for the lady of the castle. The hero agrees and asks who has imprisoned the lady. He is told that two brothers, the magicians Maboun and Yrayn, have done so, and that they are seeking to force the lady into marrying Maboun, the alternative being her death. Everyone is terrified and dare not go in, but the hero enters unafraid, with the intention of winning the lady. He enters a beautiful magic hall, where minstrels are playing. The music stops suddenly, the lights go out and the castle shakes. Then the magicians appear. The hero fights with both of them, slaying Maboun and wounding Yrayn, who then vanishes. Libeaus Desconus then sits in fear that the vanished Yrayn will perform sorcery on him, shaming him, and, as he thinks of this possibility, a snake with wings and a woman's face comes towards him.¹² It embraces and kisses him and, as soon as it does so, the snake's tail and the wings fall off, leaving the creature a wholly lovely and naked woman.¹³ The hero regrets her nakedness. She thanks him for killing her enemies, who had turned her into a snake, and tells him that her enchantment could not have ended until she had kissed Sir Gawain or one of his kin. Because he has saved her life, she will give him fifty-five castles and be his wife. Libeaus Desconus is glad, although still worried about Yrayn and what he might do.

However, all is rejoicing, the lady becomes his bride, and he returns to King Arthur, where the wedding feast lasts for forty days.

In this story, the hero explores his feelings and seeks to prove himself to himself in adventure after adventure until, at last, he succeeds. His conflicting feelings are projected outside himself, taking the form of images. He sees himself as unknown, but fair. He is unrecognized by his father, but trained for knighthood by him. Elene's male protection is reduced to a dwarf, but both these characters treat the hero as a contemptible champion. The hero then conjures up a large number of images of men and women in particular relationships with each other, and sees himself in particular relationships with them. The story is best understood if one looks, first, at the beginning and the end. At the beginning of the story, one finds the hero in sole possession of his mother, without any rival. Then, looking at the end of the story, one sees that the hero feels himself engulfed in a situation of magic and terror. He may fight, but he does not feel that he has overcome the power of the magicians. Meanwhile, the woman is seen by him as possessing a snake's tail. The lower half of her body is both bestial and phallic, filling him with horror. But, when she has embraced him, he sees her as a naked woman, her nakedness being due to his awareness that she is purely and simply a woman ready for love. Her beauty expresses her attraction for him, and all ideas of taboo have vanished. With this realization of the hero the story comes to a natural end.

In between the beginning, where the hero insists that his mother and he were all in all to each other, and the end, where he fully realizes his terror of incest and the wrath of magician fathers, the hero adventures through his feelings, testing them, and speculating. In spite of his attempts to diminish, defeat and slay male figures, some of which also represent himself, they constantly reappear, and often in the terrifying forms of black and red giants, and of magicians. Sometimes, however, they are seen as friendly, like Sir Gawain. The hero goes through a repetitive, conflicting experience of women too. They appear as scornful, then admiring; helpless and then grateful; marriageable and taboo; triumphantly beautiful and less beautiful; and as having a frightening power over men, able to take away from them everything that they value apart from a woman's love, thus leaving them contemptible. In move after move, the hero re-enacts his feelings both playfully and purposefully, and achieves a triumph which he announces to King Arthur. Then he will enter in on a further move, exploring further, related thoughts. Eventually, he visualizes himself as succumbing to 'Dame d'Amore'. He sees her as a sinister witch who has him wholly in her power. His Elene vision of woman rescues him from this vision, but only to take him on to the climax of his story where profound fears emerge. He kills one magician and causes the other to vanish, even though the fear of it still haunts him. He is now alone with the woman. He thinks of himself as the son of Sir Gawain, which acts almost like magic words, but it is expressive of something deeply important: an assertion that he is no longer unproven and un-known, but recognized by himself. At the same moment of the story, the woman expresses love for him and he experiences the contact with her which he has dreaded. Woman, who appeared as in the power of male magic; who appeared as taboo, and as possessing frightening sexual power and the power to lower and engulf him, is transformed. This is achieved by the hero's self-recognition and by his new realization, once he has dared to imagine the woman's embrace. He sees that she is beautiful, and that he can marry her. He does so, celebrating his triumph with a feast.

The transformation scene in *Libeaus Desconus* takes the form of a shape-shift, described as it takes place. The snake's tail and wings fall off the woman. In many stories, shape-shifting is an abrupt change from one image of a character to another: a heroine's beast lover suddenly ceases to be a beast and is a prince instead, and similarly the fox in *The Golden Bird* is transformed. Shape-shifting is a phenomenon arising naturally from our constantly changing experience of people. Our images of a person may change visibly, as the pictures created by our fantasy pass swiftly through our minds. The change will take place as we apprehend fresh aspects of this person, and feel that our former images have been false, or that they are, for some reason, no longer relevant or interesting. Our wishes have much to do with the changing of our images, but so have our observations of the elusive and constantly changing nature of people's moods. This seems to bring about changes in their outward appearance. The elusive and constantly changing nature of our own moods is also a vitally important factor in this process. The changing image may be an image of ourselves, as was the case in Frances' dream, and our changing moods are a fun-damental factor in our creation of images of other people. As our fantasy dramatizes our apprehensions of personality in striking images, according to how we are feeling at any particular moment, so there will be sudden changes in the images, which are equally dramatic.

Another famous story of this kind is the medieval story of the 'loathly lady', which Chaucer assigned to his Wife of Bath. It will be studied as it appears in the romance called *The Weddynge of Sir Gawen and Dame Ragnell*,[14] and in the fifteenth-century ballad *The Marriage of Sir Gawaine*.[15] This story appears to turn upon a riddle which the hero has to answer: 'What is it which women love best?'[16] The romance version begins with Arthur's hunt in a forest where he kills a hart alone. A great knight, Sir Gromer Somer Joure, appears and threatens to kill him for giving his lands to Gawain. However, the knight changes the punishment to a task, the task of discovering the answer to the riddle. Arthur has a year in which to discover the answer, and he is to return to the forest, unarmed, with it. He must keep the task a secret and he is to die if he fails to fulfil it. However, Arthur does tell Gawain, who undertakes to help the king. They travel for eleven months and fill books with answers to the riddle until Gawain thinks King Arthur is safe. However, Arthur insists upon seeking the answer once more in the forest. There he meets the hideous Dame Ragnell, riding on a gay palfrey.[17] She tells him that she knows the answer and will help, but if the answer which she gives is the right one, her reward must be marriage with Gawain. Arthur consults Gawain, and Gawain is willing to do anything to save the king. Arthur therefore receives the answer from Dame Ragnell that sovereignty over men is what women most desire, and he takes this answer to Sir Gromer. Sir Gromer is furious; it turns out that Dame Ragnell is his sister. She insists upon going to Gawain at once and marrying him openly, with a big wedding and a feast, where she wolfs her food in a manner which appalls everyone.[18] In bed, she pleads for a kiss, and Gawain courteously says that he will grant her one. Immediately she becomes very beautiful. She asks the delighted Gawain whether he would rather have her fair by night or fair by day.[19] After deliberation, Gawain gives her the choice, for he cannot come to a decision himself. The bride then declares that since she has been given the sovereignty and is 'worshyppyd', she will always be fair.[20] She explains that she was transformed by her stepmother to be ugly until the best knight in England would marry her and give her the sovereignty. After a night of love, all is explained to the rejoicing court the next day.

This is one of the most perplexing of stories. Any attempt to unravel its complexities, while, at the same time, adhering strictly to the detail given (as opposed to indulging in speculation) reveals further layers of meaning which bring one up short. But, while the story defies analysis, a study of its transformation scene cannot be omitted from this chapter, and the examination of one incident of a story necessarily involves some study of its context.

The hero appears in two acknowledged forms, Sir Gawain and King Arthur, and all the story's strange events are the creations of his mind. He appears first as the king, but it is Sir Gromer who has the sovereignty in the first part of the story. He accuses the cowed king of theft, and has him spend a year searching for the answer to a riddle, on pain of death. However, there is one who has yet more sovereignty: Sir Gromer's sister, who knows the answer to the riddle and, to her brother's fury, gives it away in return for marriage to Gawain. The subject-matter of the riddle, together with its answer, is important in itself, and so is the very fact that a riddle plays a leading rôle in the story.

Once Dame Ragnell gives the answer to the riddle, Sir Gromer is no longer significant in the story, and the events which follow are presented as being organized by her. The hero's acknowledged form, moreover, changes from being primarily that of the king to being primarily that of Gawain. While it is the hero who has cast the spell on Dame Ragnell, it is interesting to observe his sense of her power: he never bestows upon himself any initiative and does indeed give her the sovereignty. At first he sees her—and wishes to see her—as ugly: then, when he imagines her wishing for his kiss and receiving it, he immediately comes to see her as beautiful. He has, however, a sense that his vision of her must be a changeful one, and he decides to leave it to her to decide when she will seem attractive to him and when repulsive. He senses that if he loves her on her own terms she will always appear loving and lovable, and therefore beautiful; and her declaration that she will always be beautiful has the effect of magic words. Another device giving power to his greatest wishes is Dame Ragnell's explanation: she declares that the spell has been cast by her stepmother, whose power has been brought to an end by the marriage and the giving of the sovereignty to Ragnell. The idea that a stepmother caused Ragnell to appear ugly will express some of the feelings which gave rise to the hero's vision of her as ugly; and Ragnell's declaration that Gawain has now brought the lurking woman's power to an end, acts, again, as magic words. At all events, the story now comes to an end.

Before the story closes, we are told that the king and Sir Gromer become reconciled. The rôle of Sir Gromer is deeply important to the story, but while one might grasp imaginatively the nature of the feelings which conjured up the images of this knight and his hideous sister, long and close contemplation of the transformation scene itself reveals the elusive and many-sided nature of this story. It is significant that Chaucer gives it to his feminist Wife of Bath, who, it could be argued, presents us with a 'heroine' version of it.[21]

A third outstanding romance with a dénouement brought about by the processes of recognition and transformation is *Syre Gawene and the Carle of Carelyle*,[22] of which there is also a ballad version, *The Carle off Carlile*.[23] This story also contains other particularly

90

interesting features. Its events begin with a hunting expedition, during which Gawain, Kay and Bishop Baldwin seek shelter for the night in the castle of the fearsome giant, the Carl of Carlisle, who 'semyd a dredfull man'.[24] A bull, a boar, a lion and a bear are lying beside the fire and rise to attack the knights as they enter the hall, but the Carl quietens them.[25] Sir Gawain kneels courteously and the Carl bids him rise. There is a nine-gallon cup of wine from which the knights all drink, and they are well entertained. During that time, the knights leave in turn to tend their horses, and both the bishop and Kay drive away the Carl's foal from their horses, receiving a consequent blow from the Carl on their return. Gawain, however, tends the foal, as well as his own horse, and the Carl thanks him for his courtesy. The beautiful lady of the castle is admired at table by Kay, and the Carl rebukes him for this. Then the giant bids Gawain aim a spear straight at his face, and Gawain obeys, doing so with such 'ire'[26] that, as the Carl deftly lowers his head, the spear hits the wall with a force which causes it to disintegrate. Gawain now falls in love with the Carl's beautiful wife, and the Carl tells him that he must forget her because she is his, and Gawain shall not have her.[27] He has, however, a beautiful daughter too, and she sings to the harp about love and Arthur's fame. After the feast, the Carl tells Gawain to get into bed with his wife, and then orders him to kiss her.[28] However, he does not allow him to go further, interrupting Gawain's love-making. Instead, Gawain is given the beautiful daughter for the night. The next day, the Carl orders Gawain to behead him[29] and when the reluctant knight obeys, the ogre turns into a normal man of knightly aspect. He thanks Gawain for freeing him from an enchantment which could only be broken if a knight of the Round Table should behead him. He tells him, too, that, twenty years earlier, he had made a vow[30] which he had kept, to kill all those visitors to his castle who refused to obey him. Only Sir Gawain has passed the test. Showing the knight the bones of the slain, the Carl says that such things will no longer take place, and the story ends with the marriage of Gawain to the Carl's daughter and the electing of the Carl to the Round Table.

Viewed from a position outside it, this romance appears quite mystifying, but when it is viewed from a position in the mind of the hero, it begins to make sense. Indeed, the nature of the situation in which the hero finds himself is made clearer than it is in most romances by abundant detail. The morphology of the romance is peculiar in that, far from taking the form of many moves, the story is condensed, in a dreamlike fashion, the initial situation and the place of adventure becoming one. The situation is a home, in which there is a menacing, authoritative giant, a desirable woman, who is his wife, a lovely daughter, and the hero. The hero appears, at first, as three knights, the better to express the conflicting feelings which he experiences in the Carl's castle. He feels the need to express certain feelings which he also wishes to disown, and he therefore embodies them in Sir Kay and Bishop Baldwin. These two knights express that part of the hero which does not wish to please the Carl, but the hero abandons them before the important testing begins, continuing his story in the single character of Sir Gawain, which has been the aspect of the hero which wishes to please the Carl. Sir Gawain is, throughout, the acknowledged hero.

The Carl appears as a giant who is pleased if he is obeyed, and murderously angry if he is disobeyed. The atmosphere of his home is nightmarish, and, although the Carl accords reward and punishment strictly as they are merited in the foal test, his behaviour is otherwise frighteningly unpredictable and equivocal. He gives and takes away in the same breath, leaving the hero bewildered and feeling tricked. The fierce beasts which he kepts as pets, and which may be aspects of himself, wish to attack the visitors, but he quietens them. He declares himself only a 'carl', but he is the master of all. He entertains liberally and yet he never ceases to be sinister. He orders Gawain to throw a spear straight at his face, and then ducks, so that the spear is shattered against the wall—which would not have happened if the hero had not obeyed with 'ire'.

Here the hero's feelings may be discerned. He seems to have conjured up a nightmarish view of a father-figure, whom he first wishes to please. Then, under a cloak of disguises, he begins to give vent to the hostile feelings which he also harbours. He represents the father-figure as giving him extraordinary orders, which are really the hero's own wishes. He wishes to harm the father-figure and yet he does not, and the trend of his thoughts becomes clear in the scene where he finds the Carl's wife desirable. He then imagines a scene in bed with her. The Carl has, once again, 'ordered' him to act as he does, and, once again—as in the spear-throwing incident—he frustrates him. The hero sees himself as rendered powerless and sexually impotent by this father-figure every time he thinks of the mother. But his vision of the father also encompasses other aspects of his life; the ogre is seen as robbing him of all sense of power. He is seen as inviting him to attack him and then bringing about his failure. Next the hero conjures up images of this father giving him a marriageable daughter instead of his wife, and this time there is no intervention. When Gawain thinks of the daughter, the image of the ogre does not reappear. However, there must still be thoughts of taboo, and it is likely that the daughter and the mother are not wholly separate from each other in the hero's mind, for after this incident, the Carl orders Gawain to behead him. The hero is appalled at the idea which has now gripped him; he is haunted by an awareness that he is playing a dangerous game, but his wishes urge him on. What would happen if he aggressed against the Carl in this way? With an effort he performs the act in his mind and, immediately, the ogre is transformed into a friendly man. The hero has his answer and it is that nothing horrifying happens; nothing damaging to either of them results. He can do nothing damaging simply by thinking it. He realizes how wide of reality his imaginings have become, and they are no longer able to hold his belief or interest: his feelings change.

The Carl has indeed been transformed by an enchantment, as he claims, and, as he tells the hero, only Gawain's act of beheading him can break the enchantment. The hero himself has been the enchanter, putting the Carl under a spell, and hence himself too. Only he can free them both from the spell. Gawain has enjoyed the distorted images created by the enchantment but he enjoys even more, and with a sense of relief, the reassuring transformation of his images which he has achieved. The Carl is in no way diminished; he simply becomes a friendly and reasonable man—and also Gawain's father-in-law, when the hero celebrates his triumph with his marriage to the Carl's daughter.

It is now time to return to *Sir Gawain and the Green Knight*.

NOTES TO CHAPTER 7

1. Jeanne Marie, Madame Leprince de Beaumont, *Beauty and the Beast*, translated by A. E. Johnson, in *Perrault's Complete Fairy Tales* (New York, 1961), p. 115 following.

The story was previously written by Madame Gabrielle de Gallon de Villeneuve for an adult audience.

The Frog Prince, in *Grimm's Fairy Tales* (Oxford, 1962), translated by Edgar Taylor.

The story is No. 1 in the edition of Friedrich Panzer (see note 1 to Chapter 3), where it is entitled *Der Froschkönig oder der eiserne Heinrich*. In the Routledge & Kegan Paul edition (see note 1 to Chapter 3), it is also No. 1 and entitled *The Frog-King, or Iron Henry*.

See also: 'The Enchanted Pig', in *The Red Fairy Book*, edited by Andrew Lang (London, 1966), p. 104; 'East of the Sun and West of the Moon', in *The Blue Fairy Book*, edited by Andrew Lang (London, 1949), p. 24 (*The Blue Fairy Book* was the first of the collection to be published, appearing in 1889); *The Lady and the Lion*, also often called *The Singing, Soaring Lark*, No. 88 in the Grimm collection. *Snow-White and Rose-Red*, No. 161 in the Grimm collection, is another distinct story of this kind.

2. Lewis Carroll, *Alice's Adventures in Wonderland and Through the Looking-Glass*, Macmillan edition (London, 1958), p. 130 and pp. 275–81.

' "Hold your tongue!" said the Queen, turning purple.

"I won't!" said Alice.

"Off with her head!" the Queen shouted at the top of her voice. Nobody moved.

"Who cares for you?" said Alice (she had grown to her full size by this time). "You're nothing but a pack of cards!"

At this the whole pack rose up into the air . . .' (p. 130).

3. *Libeaus Desconus*, edited by M. Mills, EETS 261 (1969). The summary in this book has been made from the Cotton text.

4. *Ibid.*, Cotton text, l. 265.

5. *Ibid.*, ll. 571–9.

6. *Ibid.*, ll. 719–999.

7. *Ibid.*, ll. 1015–29.

8. *Ibid.*, l. 1400.

9. *Ibid.*, l. 1240.

10. *Ibid.*, ll. 1435–49.

11. *Ibid.*, ll. 1462–4.

12. *Ibid.*, ll. 1990–98.

13. *Ibid.*, ll. 2008–15.

14–15. 'The Weddynge of Sir Gawen and Dame Ragnell', and

'The Marriage of Sir Gawaine', both edited by W. F. Bryn and G. Dempster, in *Sources and Analogues of Chaucer's Canterbury Tales* (Chicago, 1941).

16. 'The Weddynge of Sir Gawen and Dame Ragnell', l. 91.

17. *Ibid.*, ll. 225–49.

18. *Ibid.*, ll. 608–19.

19. *Ibid.*, ll. 656–65.

20. *Ibid.*, ll. 685–9.

21. *The Poetical Works of Chaucer*, edited by F. N. Robinson (London), pp. 101–6; *The Canterbury Tales*, translated into modern English by Nevill Coghill (Penguin Books, 1951), pp. 297–308.

22–23. 'Syre Gawene and the Carle of Carelyle' and 'The Carle off Carlile', both edited by A. Kurvinen in *Annales Academiae Scientiarum Fennicae* (Helsinki, 1951).

There is a translation of this story into Modern English by Elisabeth Brewer in *From Cuchulainn to Gawain: Sources and Analogues of Sir Gawain and the Green Knight* (Cambridge, 1973).

24. 'Syre Gawene and the Carle of Carelyle', p. 249.

25. *Ibid.*, ll. 223–34.

26. *Ibid.*, ll. 394.

27. *Ibid.*, ll. 409–14.

28. *Ibid.*, ll. 448–56.

29. The beheading scene only occurs in 'The Carle off Carlile', and, in her edition of the texts, Miss Kurvinen shows that both the surviving versions of the story are derivatives of an earlier tail-rhyme romance, now lost. She suggests that the absence of the beheading scene in 'Syre Gawene and the Carle of Carelyle' (the Porkington text), while it appears in the later ballad, may have been due to the loss of a folio from the scribe's manuscript.

30. The Carl's explanation of a vow only appears in 'Syre Gawene and the Carle of Carelyle', and it serves as a rationalization in lieu of the explanation of the enchantment which appears in 'The Carle off Carlile'.

8 Sir Gawain and the Green Knight

SIR GAWAIN IS enjoying the New Year festivities at King Arthur's court when his adventure with the Green Knight begins. The feast is described in great detail, and the atmosphere of happiness and good feeling which this conveys is paramount in the story. Equally celebrated is the splendour of the company, particularly that of the King and Queen. Guinevere, 'ful gay'[1] in the midst of the company, and next to whom Sir Gawain is sitting, is described first:

> ... 'Fairest of form was this queen,
> Glinting and grey of eye;
> No man could say he had seen
> A lovelier but with a lie.'[2]

Arthur, described immediately afterwards, is young, merry, boyish and restless: he will not eat until told a new and marvellous story of adventure about ancestors or arms, or until he is given a strong opponent for an actual combat. Just as the first course is served, the Green Knight enters.

To begin with, it is the King, rather than Sir Gawain, who expresses a desire for marvels and combat. It is only after Arthur has accepted the Green Knight's challenge that his adventure becomes that of Sir Gawain. He is Gawain's uncle, and, while there is no reason why he should not appear as young as he does, the way in which he appears suggests that he represents the hero, to some extent, at this point of the story. Presumably, he is seated on the other side of the Queen from Sir Gawain. The latter is silent, until he begs that the game may be his. There may be more than one important reason why the hero has chosen to appear as the King until after the Green Knight's challenge has been taken up. Meanwhile, 'good Gawain', seated in silence next to the Queen, is also experienced by participators in the story as the hero.

In one hand the Green Knight carries a huge axe, and in the other a holly bough, the natural and colourful greenery of winter. This equivocal figure suggests a Christmas game, in which a knight should deal him a blow with the axe and then receive a return blow from the Green Knight a year later. The hero desires this game, although he also feels that the contest must be an unequal one—

and no less unequal or sinister for his having the first blow. The image of the Green Knight has been conjured up as a result of his own wishes, and is a product of his own feelings, and yet the hero is conscious only that an exciting and horrifying adventure has come upon him from somewhere outside himself. He does not know who the Green Knight is, and yet, somewhere in his mind, he is aware that he is someone significant whom he wishes to encounter in the fashion which he has devised.

Thus the hero creates a drama which he presents to himself, and to us all, as one in which he becomes involved by chance, and owing to his knightly courage. This is how he wishes to see it. That it represents a conflict of feelings within him and takes place entirely in his own mind from beginning to end he would never believe. His wishes overcoming his fears, he takes up the axe and chops off the Green Knight's head. He has not introduced the idea of beheading into the Green Knight's challenge, which simply speaks of blows, but when the time comes for Gawain's blow to be struck, the assumption is that this is to be a beheading. The severed head rolls gruesomely on the floor and the hero enjoys the horror of it for a moment. Then his beheaded monster rises and picks up his head which, held up high, reminds Gawain of his side of the bargain. He will find the place where he is to receive his return blow by asking his way, for the Knight is well-known as the Knight of the Green Chapel. No directions to this place are given, and, later, it transpires that none are needed, for Sir Gawain knows how to find it.

At this stage of the story, all that participators in the story are conscious of, where the Green Chapel is concerned, is that it is a profoundly significant place. The Green Knight's very identification of himself as the Knight of the Green Chapel conveys its central importance in the story, and the fact that the return blow is to be dealt there strengthens one's sense of its importance. Moreover, the fact that the two parts of the game both take place at New Year deepens one's sense of the connection between them. There must be a link in the hero's mind between the Green Chapel and the situation, as he sees it, at King Arthur's court. The Green Chapel is clearly integral with the feelings which give rise to the Green Knight, and must therefore have been in the hero's thoughts from the moment when he first desires adventure. Also in his thoughts when he first desires adventure are the joy and splendour of the feast, the surpassing beauty of the Queen, and the fun-loving adventurousness of the King. Finally, it will also be important that Sir Gawain beheads the Green Knight at King Arthur's court while he himself is to be beheaded in return at the Green Chapel.

The Green Knight's beheading is not about death, and one senses that that of Sir Gawain may not be about death either. The actual experience of the beheading scene, however—and it is given significant attention—suggests that it is about something sinister and gruesome, while, at the same time, we never lose sight of the feeling that this is all, indeed, no more than a game. However, game or not, it is an engagement surrounded by lurking doubts about the hero's safety: it is believed that the Green Knight survives unscathed because he is magical, while Sir Gawain does not possess any such magical power. At this point, it must be recalled that the Green Knight is not himself the possessor of the magical power: while we have not yet been given the explanation that the Knight has been enchanted by Morgan the Fay, it is apparent that, if this is a story, the hero is the source of the magic and will have brought about the Green Knight's enchantment. However, while the magic is the hero's own, its source is in his wishes, which he senses to be omnipotent, but which are also in conflict with each other. This is how it comes about that the hero's own created story takes the form of an exciting and terrifying speculation: what will happen as a result of his beheading of the Green Knight? The hero's own wishes and other feelings impel the story while leaving him without a sense of full control over what is to happen next.

The journey through the wintry wilderness expresses the hero's state of mind as he proceeds with his speculation. He, and all those of us who have joined him in his story, do not, significantly, yet have much idea as to the full nature of the feelings which have given rise to the story. The hero is engaged in a searching exploration of them. In the wilderness, he experiences an icy chill, in sharp contrast to the friendly warmth of the festive court, and this mood is aggravated by a sense that he is alone and far from his friends, while continually being attacked by enemies—wild beasts, ogres and dragons—which have to be overcome.

However, he cannot remain in the wilderness for ever. His mood must change. He thinks of Christmas and rides into a forest. Suddenly a beautiful castle appears and he is given the warmest welcome there. In the castle are a lord, his fair lady and a hideous old woman whom everyone respects. The Christmas hospitality there, the fun, feasting and blazing fires, express the new feeling which has come over the hero, in total contrast to the wilderness feelings. The change from the wintry wilderness of anxiety to the warmth of love is all the more forcible for the fact that in the latter mood can be seen a clear parallel to the mood at the beginning of the romance. It is also expressed in similar imagery to that expressing the mood at Arthur's castle, and this makes it all the more evident that Sir Gawain's story has entered upon a new move.

The main characters belonging to the first castle had been Sir Gawain's uncle King Arthur, the fair Guinevere, and the hero. In this second castle, we find a lord as jovial as Arthur, a fair lady and a hideous older woman of high rank. Just as a game was played in the last castle, there is also a game played in this, a game within a game, for the culmination of the first game is fast approaching. This second game is, on the face of it, a very different game from the first. The hero arranges that it will involve three people, the lord, the lady and himself, and that, in strong contrast to the first game, it will be played on a highly sophisticated level. In it the hero also acts out his feelings much more explicitly, and it is for this purpose that he has brought himself to this second castle. The lord and lady are separated, the lord sent out hunting in the forest, and the lady staying at home with Gawain, who arranges to be the only man to stay behind from the hunt. He is to be in bed instead. Of course, he also goes out on the hunt with the lord, and the events which he conjures up there are deeply important to the story. They are an expression of his feelings as he lies in bed and has the lady make love to him. The main feeling which he acknowledges as he lies in bed is embarrassment, but his enjoyment is also paramount in the dalliance which takes place. He has had much to arrange in order to give this game its almost carefree fun. Above all, it is presented as organized by the lord and the lady of the castle, who are themselves under the orders of Morgan the Fay. The game is also separated into two parts, the lady's side of it being presented, at the time, as not a game at all but a result of the lady's own private wishes. The hero goes through the defence of projection, giving his wishes to the lady and ultimately to Morgan the Fay, and, at the same time, disguising the nature of the game by splitting off the central aspect of it. This central aspect is also explained, eventually, as having been a test, and it is felt to be a test at the time. Sir Gawain really feels tested, particularly because his need for reassurance that he is not harming his host is so great that he has to believe that he has no wish to do so. These feelings are put into action by his keeping his side of the bargain in giving the lord the kisses which the lady gives him. This exchange bargain is the most obvious link between the two parts of the game, but the very character of the hunts and the hunted links them profoundly to the scenes in the bedchamber, as has already been observed, perhaps most penetratingly by John Speirs.[3] Charles Moorman[4] points out the clear parallels between the two Christmas games themselves: the slaughtering of the captured animals suggests the beheading game, and the exchange of gifts at the end of each day suggests the exchange of blows. He was looking for parallels throughout the romance to demonstrate its structural unity, but here he came nearer to a profound comment on the story than he perhaps realized.

While Sir Gawain lies in bed enjoying dalliance with the lady, he is also out in the wintry wilderness taking part in the hunt. He conjures up images of a ferocious hunt of female deer on the edge of a forest, during which many of the helpless creatures are killed when arrows pierce their flesh. These does have been separated from their harts, which are not being hunted, and, always timorous, they are now terrified. As Sir Gawain pictures this scene he conjures up the lady creeping to his bed, where he lies quivering. When she is sitting on his bed, a conversation of courtly elegance is invented, but it makes no real attempt to hide the primal feelings in the hero's mind. He has the lady offer her body to him, praising him in fulsome terms and telling him how much she loves him. He himself assumes an all-virtuous front, admitting to no wishes and to no love for the lady. It is she, and not he, who suggests a kiss and he 'allows' her one, but not before he has thought of the blow of the axe. He sends the lady out and rises to enjoy the company of all the ladies, particularly that of the beautiful young one and the mysterious old one. Then he turns his mind fully to the hunt again, imagining the beheading, chopping up, and disemboweling of the female deer, followed by the lord's triumphant return to the blazing fires of the castle. There he gives the flesh of his quarry to Gawain and Gawain gives the lord the kiss of his quarry. There is a melding of the quarry, and, to a certain extent, a melding of the two men. The picture has been rather confused, for the simple reason that the hero's mind is in a state of confusion. He has seen the lord as all powerful over 'female deer', and he has also seen him as a slayer of timid animals, with which the hero has identified to a certain extent in his first scene with the lady. At the same time, Gawain has seen himself also as a hunter of female quarry, and he sees his powers in this respect as thrilling, frightening and harmful. However, the meeting, exchange and festivities reassure Gawain. The rather frightening feelings which he has experienced come to be seen by him as no more than some flesh and a kiss, and all is made above-board and open, with the festive exchange.

But the hero wishes to renew his thoughts of the lady. The lord is sent out hunting again, without a specified quarry until he and his men reach a quagmire in the forest. There, a vast boar suddenly leaps out of the bushes, and it seems insuperable. There is a fearsome fight with it, and the hero's thoughts leave this fight in full swing in order to conjure up another vision of the lady. He has her return to his bedside and tell him that he can take her by force if he wishes. He then has her add that this need only happen if she is so ill-bred as to resist. The conversation takes on its now customary courtly artificiality, which, nevertheless, does not hide the warmly human feelings which are being given play at the same time. The conversation is about kissing, but the hero defends himself against there being any physical love-making on his part, 'allowing' the lady to give him only two kisses. He then has her depart and turns his mind to safer images of his enjoyment of the feminine company which he feels is more permissible. But he does not dwell on this scene; his thoughts quickly fly to the battle with the boar. The terrible creature has wounded many men and hounds, but, growing tired, it now rushes towards a hole by a running stream, and the lord approaches it as it stands with its back to the bank, scraping. It springs out at the lord, and the two adversaries fight in the stream until the lord, at last, kills the boar. Its head is then cut off and its body cut up, before the hunters return in triumph with the boar's head borne in front of the lord. This head is given to Sir Gawain and the hero gives the lady's two kisses to her husband, in exchange. He expresses his horror at the sight of his host's quarry, now given to him to be his instead of the kisses. The evening is, however, festive and all is reassurance once more, in spite of the confused and conflicting feelings still battling in the hero's mind. The lord has beheaded the ferocious beast which attacked him, and Gawain sees himself as that ferocious beast. It is both horrifying and reassuring that this aspect of himself has been vanquished and beheaded. The hero both wants and does not want to be this beast in the lord's forest, and he sees his bedroom thoughts as a thrilling but very dangerous game. As the exchange takes place, the two men seem to meld a little again; the lord is not wholly a rival, even though there is an unmistakable link between him and the Green Knight, for there is something of Gawain in him. To a considerable extent, the hero himself deliberately vanquishes his ferocious beast aspect, as he arranges for the lord to do it. As the boar's head and and the two kisses meet, in the exchange, the hero is able to create another scene of wit and festivity, but there cannot be complete reassurance for the hero. The feelings which he is enjoying are beginning to become a little too frightening again. However, the images of the boar's head and the kisses leave his mind at the subsequent feast, when he enjoys voluptuous thoughts of the lady who, he continues to maintain, is bewitching him.

Then Gawain thinks of a fox. The lord pursues this cunning animal until, full of fear and woe, it makes for the woods where it is called a thief and threatened. It, nevertheless, leads them all a dance, wheeling back into the woods every time the huntsmen succeed in chasing it out into the open. As the hero thinks of this, he conjures up the lady again, their situation together being once more that of his being in bed while she is at his bedside. She is, however, no longer fully clothed; this time, he has stripped her so

101

that her breasts and back are bare as she makes her advances. He cannot enjoy his arousal without thoughts of the Green Knight and a deep feeling of peril, but he has the lady swoop over him, laughing seductively, to kiss him. He gazes at her and her attire with rapture, and he allows himself to dwell on tempting thoughts until he can scarcely resist. As he has the lady speak the words for which he longs, the lord is still in pursuit of the thieving fox, which Sir Gawain pictures as both enjoying a game and feeling dismayed. He resists his tempting thoughts, announcing that he does not wish for there to be any woman in his life at present. Thereupon, he has the lady kiss him again and ask for the gift of a glove. He resists both this overture and the subsequent one of her offer of a gold ring. Then he thinks of the lady offering him the gift of a green girdle which will protect him from death.

So far, the hero has admitted to his delight and to his terror that he will betray the lord. He admits only to being the passive receiver of kisses from the lady, but whatever he may choose to tell of the events in the bedchamber, his thoughts have been very different from those which he claims to have, and they have immediately become deeds in his mind. He and the lady lie together in his thoughts and therefore in deed, and meanwhile his image of the magical Green Knight haunts him and melds with his image of the lord. Gawain's terror springs from his belief that his thoughts and wishes have omnipotent powers; and it has become apparent in the story that while some of his thoughts and wishes are in his favour, others are not. Gawain thinks, for instance, that he should be punished for some of his wishes. Thus he cannot rely on the wishes which wish him well and he wonders how he can get control over the magic. The solution, he feels, is in the possession of a tangible magical object which he can trust to be single-mindedly in his favour. This should be a gift from his lady, because, in firmly expressing her love for him, it will reinforce the power of those wishes which are in his favour. He also feels that in expressing the lady's love for him, it will give him a sense of the rightness of this love and thus allay those feelings of his which are against him. It is for such reasons that Gawain brings about the gift of the Green Girdle, which he feels will protect him from the Green Knight. He then has the lady kiss him again, and thinks of himself rising to make merry with the ladies—and to confess his sins in the chapel.

However his thoughts return to the hunting field, only to see the fox rush through a thicket and bound out to face the lord, standing there awaiting him with his sword. Swerving to avoid the sword, as it is drawn, the fox is set upon by the waiting hounds and, totally outwitted, he is, in no time, reduced to a piece of skin. This skin is given to Gawain, but Gawain gives the lord only the lady's three kisses, and not the green girdle. The green girdle is, nonetheless, present in the images during the exchange scene. As the hero looks at the red skin, which is all that remains of a creature which has tried to outwit the lord, and which now belongs to him, thoughts of the green girdle are in his mind. It is being held back from its rightful recipient because it represents to him the lady's love for himself and will, as a result, give him greater power to pit against his Green Knight feelings. But as he hopes this, his terror of the Green Knight is overwhelming him. The sight of the fox's skin and the knowledge that he has withheld the girdle are no reassurance whatever, and frightened goodbyes cloud the feast that evening.

The next morning, Sir Gawain is in the wintry wilderness again. He ties the lady's girdle round his own loins, as if to protect them, and sets off in his mind to meet the Green Knight. He is given a 'guide' but he has no need for one. He knows that the Green Knight dwells in the midst of his icy wilderness mood, and by the Green Chapel. The guide is that part of him which tells him that the tryst is too terrifying to face, that the Green Knight attacks all men who go near the Chapel, and that no one need know if Gawain decides not to go to it after all. But this is an aspect of himself which the hero is able to discard. Terrified as he is, he wishes to complete his exploration of his feelings and to follow through his speculation as to what will be the outcome of his adventure: he wishes to experience the adventure to the full. He conjures up the image of the Green Chapel, when he has discarded the 'guide', and sees it as a mound over a cave, with a hole in each end and on either side, and overgrown with grass in great patches. Having looked around it and said that it looks like a place of worship for the Devil, being the most cursed church which he has ever entered, he roams up to its roof, with his high helmet on his head, and holding his lance. From that height, he immediately hears the sharpening of an axe. The image of the Green Knight has followed upon his thoughts of the Green Chapel, sharpening an axe ready to inflict the punishment which the hero associates with the thoughts which he is entertaining. His contemplation of the delight and, for him, the terror of sex gives rise to a series of grandiose pictures which are both detailed and disguised. The pictures can be seen to parallel those where the fox rushes through a thicket and bounds out to find the lord waiting for him, sword in hand. The fox is killed, but at the Green Chapel the outcome is different. The Green Knight's punishment is conjured up, and the terror is prolonged by two suspended blows, because, the hero tells us, he is afraid. Fear, however, is apparently not Gawain's only experience at this moment. The axe swings down savagely for the third time and the wound is but slight.

Gawain has realized something which has weakened the power of the Green Knight. He springs up, and the Green Knight ceases to appear as the Green Knight; he is revealed as the lord of the castle. Gawain experiences astonishment, but it has been clear earlier in his story that he has been unconsciously aware, all the time, that the two knights are linked in his mind. Something has happened in Sir Gawain's mind which has averted the terrible punishment, and made the Green Knight vanish, in favour of the lord of the castle. What has occurred to bring about this transformation?

Whenever he thinks about woman, Sir Gawain sees her as, in some way, taboo. She only actually appears in an obvious triangle situation including the hero, in the second move, with the appearance of the lord and lady of the castle. But this couple parallels the royal couple, to whom the hero is nephew, in the first move. As so often in story, the second move clarifies the situation which exists in the hero's mind in the first move of his story. Its characters reveal more about how the hero sees those in his initial situation; and its events—in this case the second game—reveal the nature of the hero's conflicts. The disguises, however, are deep. We are not told what the Green Chapel looks like until the climax of the story, and it is not until the lord of the castle 'explains' the whole adventure to Sir Gawain, that we learn much about the intriguing old woman living with him. He then reveals that she is Morgan the Fay, the witch, and Gawain's own aunt. She, the lord says, has planned the whole affair, using her powers of magic gained from her lover, Merlin, to transform the lord of the castle into the Green Knight. The confusing fragmentation of characters is no longer so confusing, although it still reveals confusion in the hero's mind. Behind all the magic lurk a pair of lovers invested with magical powers: Merlin and Morgan the Fay. The investing of magical powers in parents is a normal phenomenon in children, and deep at the roots of Sir Gawain's adventure lurk such magical parents. There are also Arthur and Guinevere, who appear as a young couple, and yet who are really uncle and aunt to the hero. Arthur, when he longs for an adventure and then is enraged by the Green Knight, appears as an aspect of the hero, but he also appears as a king. There is a similar confusion of generations where the lord and lady of the castle are concerned. They are a young couple, but the hero also links them in his mind with the Green Knight and the old woman—even as they also appear in clear contrast to the latter characters.

Why does the fascinating Morgan the Fay appear as a hideous old woman in this romance—especially as her brother, King Arthur, appears as a young man? She is seen as repulsive, while her enchantments are experienced by the hero in the form of a beautiful young woman, whose beauty expresses desirability. Nevertheless, in spite of this disguise of displacement, and the defence of her hideous appearance, the enchantments are still those of Morgan the Fay. It is significant that Morgan the Fay is Gawain's aunt, as is also Guinevere, loveliest of women. The two women must be one woman in the hero's mind, but at the castle he represses the identity of Morgan the Fay so that he does not know who she is. This would explain the extraordinary fact that aunt and nephew spend Christmas together while Gawain remains unaware of their relationship. Only when Gawain feels able to do so does he acknowledge Morgan the Fay's identity. Then we are specifically told that it is this woman's magic which is the cause of the whole adventure.

What exactly has given rise to the particular characteristics of the images of the Green Knight and the Green Chapel, and what happens when they are finally conjured up together at the climax of Sir Gawain's adventure?

All is contrast in this romance. Of the two games, one is violent and the other is played on the most sophisticated level, all its undercurrents of feeling regulated into the strict forms of chivalry and hunting. The striking images springing from the hero's conflicting feelings all show evocative contrast: the green ogre and the genial lord; the beautiful young woman and the hideous old one; the splendid feasts and the wintry wildernesses; savagery and the height of culture; magic and the natural. We feel the contrast, too, between warmth and freezing cold; red fires and a white landscape; the red berries against the green of the holly, and the Green Knight's blood against the green of his skin. But the contrast is more subtle than this. There is a sinister difference between the red and green of the holly, and the red and green of the beheaded knight. What is it? There is something horrifying about the knight's being green; why? When asked this question, an eleven-year-old boy, Kenneth, gave an immediate and telling answer: 'Because it's the colour that people aren't.'[5] In this answer are contained the essential reasons why the Knight is green. While holly is green by nature, the Knight is not, and it is more wholly unnatural that he should be green than it would be if he were any other colour. The Green Knight's colour emphasizes that he cannot exist in nature; he cannot exist in the outer world of reality. The Green Chapel sounds equally unnatural, but when it is actually encountered and is seen to have the form of a grassy mound, the green is no longer felt to be unnatural. It is the name 'chapel' which is wholly inappropriate, and its use must express the way in which the hero sees that which it represents. The hero sees woman's sexuality as a chapel and, with green as its colour, it is proclaimed as lurid and unnatural. All that is really in the hero's mind is taboo, and when woman's sexuality is finally visualized at the climax of the story, it is symbolized, not by a chapel, but by an object which is certainly not taboo and which is quite naturally green. The story has, among its other intentions, been a reassurance fulfilment: it is the dissipation of the fantasies, upon the recognition of their total unreality, which brings about this reassurance.

The lady's girdle is also green, and, as such, contrasts with the redness of the fox's skin, for which it should have been exchanged. At that stage of his story, the hero is still thinking of green as the colour of those things which are magical, such as the Green Knight and the Green Chapel, and thus the girdle, invested with magical powers, appears as green. Later, at the end of his story, the girdle is felt to be natural, as the Green Chapel has proved to be, and, like the Chapel, remains naturally green, just as the fox's pelt is naturally red. He arranges that the lord announces his personal ownership of the girdle (owing to its having been woven by his wife) and then transfers this ownership to himself, saying that he gives him the gold-hemmed girdle, for it is green like his gown. Thus the ownership of the girdle is expressly handed over to the hero, and, at this very moment, the magical associations which have haunted its colour green are no longer felt to be present. The Green Knight himself has become a friendly man who refers only to the green colour of his clothing: there is no longer any unnatural greenness about his appearance. His generous presentation of the girdle to the hero expresses an important realization on the hero's part. In the scene of the third exchange at the lord's castle he has had a vision of two trophies: one the displayed fox's skin which expresses his apprehension of the power of the lord's hatred for him, and the other the hidden green girdle which expresses his feeling of the power of the lady's love for him. Now this girdle is bestowed upon him willingly by the lord and it is both changed in significance and no longer magical. When Sir Gawain wears it at King Arthur's court, he proclaims that it is the sign of his perfidy, and that it is being worn as a penance, but he arranges that all King Arthur's knights shall wear it, and all his protestations are overwhelmed by his feeling of its deep importance, its honourable importance, to all men.

The contrast between the green colour of the Knight and the green colour of the Chapel pinpoints the conflict of the hero. He must succeed in recognizing the fact that the Green Chapel is quite natural, whereas the Green Knight is not. His giving both images the colour green expresses this realization deep in his mind, but his feelings are struggling in profound conflict. All these feelings are as natural as the Green Chapel, but the hero cannot accept some of them, and their conflict disturbs him to such an extent that his images take quite unreal forms—especially owing to his belief that his feelings have powers of magical proportions. Somewhere in his mind he knows that this belief in magical powers is nonsense and that all this will prove to be an illusion. There is a genuine and profound battle between his feelings, but it is all also a game during which the hero explores and plays with his feelings. He has the axe threaten him three times, as he plays even with the horrifying idea of the punishment which he compulsively thinks of whenever he thinks of the Green Chapel.

The hideous punishment never takes place, for it is at this moment that the hero realizes the full meaning of what he saw when he conjured up the images of the Green Knight and the Green Chapel side by side. The latter, visualized first, appears in a form which belies all that its name suggests, consequently also belying the existence of a Green Knight. Having seen the Green Chapel in a natural light, the hero no longer feels that a Green Knight is relevant to it. It cannot be so. For this reason, the image vanishes at once, being replaced by a more natural image.

At this moment of his story, under the swing of the axe, Gawain metes out to himself the rewards and punishments which he feels are his due. Having realized that his thoughts merit very little in the way of punishment, he is untouched by the first two blows and then receives only a nick in the neck for accepting the green girdle during the third temptation scene, without honestly returning it to the lord. Here he has been a thief, like the fox, but he sees now that this is not too serious an offence and merits only a small punishment. He feels ashamed, however, at his dishonesty and cowardice.

Sir Gawain also has other reasons for feeling ashamed at this time. As recognition comes, he realizes that his mind has played a trick on him. The images have been thrilling and horrifying, and also a joke—his own joke, with which he has hood-winked himself. His feelings are mixed as this recognition comes. The enchantments vanish, and he feels that he should be punished a little for ever having believed in them: he has, however, succeeded in dissolving them at the moment when he feels this to be essential for continued enjoyment of his story. The paramount feelings following upon the transformation scene are those of good feeling towards himself and a sense of triumph. The lord of the castle expresses the good feeling, while the acclaim of King Arthur's court expresses the triumph. Such good feelings are primary throughout this festival poem: they are ever-present as Sir Gawain explores his emotional experiences from the nightmare to the feast.

1. *Sir Gawain and the Green Knight*, edited by J. R. R. Tolkien and E. V. Gordon (Oxford, 1925), l. 74.

2. *Sir Gawain and the Green Knight*, translated by Brian Stone, p. 26.

3. John Speirs, 'Sir Gawain and the Green Knight' in *Scrutiny*, Vol. 16, No. 4 (1949), p. 290.

4. Charles Moorman, 'Myth and Medieval Literature: Sir Gawain and the Green Knight', in *Sir Gawain and Pearl: Critical Essays*, edited by R. J. Blanch (Indiana, 1966), p. 122.

5. Kenneth Brockington Wilson, September 1973.

Conclusion

A STUDENT OF stories must always be exploring and always gaining new insights, for this subtle and ultimately equivocal form of art will, by its very nature, always keep us guessing. The very nature of stories is, of course, a reflection of the minds which produce them, and the more we grasp their many-sided character and intentions, and the nature of the thinking which brings them into being, the more we can learn about the place from which they have sprung: ourselves. The fact that the answers to our questions will always be somewhat like the answers given to Macbeth by the Weird Sisters makes our exploration endlessly intriguing.

Analysis can be a destructive process, but the elusiveness of stories gives them an indestructible power. Our analyses can only appear lame beside the impact of the stories themselves: art embodies the profound and complex conceptions of the imagination, expressed in its appropriate language, while we are confined to the, here, inappropriate conceptual powers and language of the intellect. A few images convey the full reality of the mind's contents at any single moment of time, while the critic's grasp of such realities must always be only partial and further limited by the cumbersome and inadequate language of words.

In spite of the necessary limitations of this study, many important factors have emerged. If we approach a story by joining the story-teller and his acknowledged hero by identification, and thus view the story as the creation of the 'hero', who represents us all, we see all the events of the story in a context which reveals them to be decidedly meaningful. Seen as thoughts in the mind of the hero, all the elements of a story link together to convey definite, albeit ambiguous, significance. This significance is grasped by our unconscious minds, making possible the accurate transmission of stories which has preserved them as they have been preserved. In order to grasp this significance consciously, we have to be able to enter into the kind of thinking which creates the story. It is essentially magical, conflicting, changeful and disguised, and it spontaneously expresses itself through a language of pictures. This pictorial language is not formalized, like the language of words. It will mean only what the hero wishes it to mean at any given moment of his story and his wishes may be in opposition to each other at that moment. Every story is unique and must be studied in isolation from other stories, once we have given deep thought to the nature of the entire genre to which it belongs. Every story must be studied in its entirety: there can be no detail which is not meaningful.

In this book, the 'genre' has been considered only as folktale and romance. There has been no investigation of stories usually classified as myth, legend, fable, fabliau, science-fiction, detective story or novel. These forms of story are all different in certain important respects from the stories which have been studied, but research might discover that the findings of this present study have limited relevance to some examples of these other forms of story.

Of all forms of story, the novel appears to be the most distinct in this respect. Essentially, the great novelist distances himself from his material and thinks about it rationally, with many more concerns in mind than has the creator of romance and folktale. With his interest in the outer world and his attainment of a measure of detachment from himself, the great novelist develops his characters into personalities which resemble people as they are in actuality, and the circumstances in which they are placed throughout the novel are governed by interests in the creator's mind other than his personal wishes. There is, in fact, a conscious, intellectual control governing the entire imaginative creation. This achievement is, however, not always evident in works known as 'novels': such works as Charlotte Brontë's *Jane Eyre* appear to have some of the characteristics of a romance.

The approach to story undertaken in this book will not be the only valid approach but it is one through which, with our own individual insights, we can make many illuminating discoveries. Perhaps, above all, the romance and traditional tale will come to be recognized as an experience where mind meets mind at many levels of knowing, and where both dream and reality are celebrated in a 'festive moment' which is often raised to a 'timeless feast'.[1]

1. K. Kerényi, *The Religion of the Greeks and Romans* (London, 1962), p. 65.

Select Bibliography

PRIMARY MATERIALS

Amis and Amiloun, edited by MacEdward Leach, Early English Text Society 203 (1937).

Brer Rabbit and Brer Fox, retold by Jane Shaw, from the original of Joel Chandler Harris (London, 1969).

'The Carle off Carlile', edited by A. Kurvinen, in *Annales Academiae Scientiarum Fennicae* (Helsinki, 1951).

Lewis Carroll, *Alice's Adventures in Wonderland and Through the Looking-Glass*, Macmillan edition (London, 1958).

F. C. Child, *English and Scottish Popular Ballads*, edited by H. C. Sargent and G. L. Kittredge (London, 1904).

Clariodus, published in Edinburgh (1830). Presented to the Members of the Maitland Club by Edward Piper.

Eger and Grime, edited by J. R. Caldwell (Harvard, 1933).

Geraldine Elliot, Books of Malawian Folk Tales: *The Long Grass Whispers* (London, 1939); *Where the Leopard Passes* (London 1949); *The Hunter's Cave* (London, 1951); and *The Singing Chameleon* (London, 1957).

Emare, edited by Edith Ricket, EETS ES 99 (1906).

Sir Gawain and the Green Knight, edited by J. R. R. Tolkien and E. V. Gordon (Oxford, 1925).

Sir Gawain and the Green Knight, edited by R. A. Waldron (London, 1970).

Sir Gawain and the Grene Gome, prepared and introduced by R. T. Jones (London, 1972).

Sir Gawain and the Green Knight, translated by Brian Stone (Penguin Books, 1959).

'Syre Gawene and the Carle of Carelyle', edited by A. Kurvinen, in *Annales Academiae Scientiarum Fennicae* (Helsinki, 1951).

Die Kinder- und Hausmärchen der Brüder Grimm, vollständige Ausgape in der Urfassung, herausgegeben von Friedrich Panzer (Wiesbaden, c. 1950).

Jacob and Wilhelm Grimm, *Grimm's Fairy Tales,* translated by Edgar Taylor (Oxford, 1962).

Grimm's Fairy Tales, complete edition based on the translation of Margaret Hunt and thoroughly revised, corrected and completed by James Stern (Routledge & Kegan Paul, 1948).

Homer: The Odyssey, translated by E. V. Rieu (Penguin Books, 1946).

King Horn, edited by Joseph Hall (Oxford, 1901).

Andrew Lang, *The Blue Fairy Book* (London, 1949).

Andrew Lang, *The Red Fairy Book* (London, 1966).

Libeaus Desconus, edited by M. Mills, EETS 261 (1969).

Les Lais de Marie de France, edited by Jean Rychner (Paris, 1966).

'The Marriage of Sir Gawaine', edited by W. F. Bryan and G. Dempster in *Sources and Analogues of Chaucer's Canterbury Tales* (Chicago, 1941).

The Book of Narrative Poetry, compiled by John R. Crossland (London, 1937).

The Oxford Book of Ballads, edited by Arthur Quiller-Couch (Oxford, 1920).

The Oxford Book of Ballads, edited by James Kinsley (Oxford, 1969).

Perrault's Complete Fairy Tales, translated by A. E. Johnson and others (New York, 1961).

Tristan und Isolde, by Gottfried von Strassburg, edited by Wolfgang Golther (Berlin and Stuttgart, 1888), 2 vols.

Les Fragments du Roman de Tristan par Thomas, edited by Bartina H. Wind (Leiden, 1950).

Beroul: The Romance of Tristan, translated by Alan S. Fedrick (Penguin Books Ltd, 1970).

Gottfried von Strassburg's Tristan, with the surviving fragments of the Tristan of Thomas, translated by A. T. Hatto (Penguin Books Ltd, 1960).

'The Weddynge of Sir Gawen and Dame Ragnell', edited by W. F. Bryan and G. Dempster, in *Sources and Analogues of Chaucer's Canterbury Tales* (Chicago, 1941).

SECONDARY MATERIALS

A STORY-TELLING AND LITERARY TECHNIQUE

1. General works

Elizabeth Cook, *The Ordinary and the Fabulous* (Cambridge, 1969).

Ruth Finnegan, *Oral Literature in Africa* (Oxford, 1970).

Laura A. Hibbard, *Medieval Romance in England* (New York and Oxford, 1924).

Laura Hibbard Loomis, *Adventures in the Middle Ages* (New York, 1962).

Norman N. Holland, *The Dynamics of Literary Response* (New York, 1968).

Antony Jones and June Buttrey, *Children and Stories* (Oxford, 1970).

R. S. Loomis, *Celtic Myth and Arthurian Romance* (New York, 1927).

Albert B. Lord, *The Singer of Tales* (Harvard and London, 1960).

P. M. Pickard, *I Could a Tale Unfold* (London, 1961).

Vladimir Propp, 'Morphology of the Folktale', in *International Journal of American Linguistics*, Vol. 24, No. 4 (October 1958).

H. J. Rose, *A Handbook of Greek Mythology* (London, 1928).

J. Burke Severs, *A Manual of the Writings in Middle English, 1050–1500*, Vol. 1 (New Haven, Connecticut, 1967).

John Speirs, *Medieval English Poetry: The Non-Chaucerian Tradition* (London, 1957).

Eugène Vinaver, *The Rise of Romance* (Oxford, 1971).

Jessie L. Weston, *From Ritual to Romance* (Cambridge, 1920).

2. Special studies

A. C. Baugh, 'Improvisation in the Middle English Romance', in *The Proceedings of the American Philosophical Society*, Vol. 103 (1959).

D. E. Baughan, 'The Role of Morgan le Fay in Sir Gawain and the Green Knight', in *ELH*, Vol. 17, p. 241 (1949).

Larry D. Benson, *Art and Tradition in Sir Gawain and the Green Knight* (New Brunswick, N.J., 1965).

Robert J. Blanch (ed.), *Sir Gawain and Pearl: Critical Essays* (Indiana, 1966).

J. Bolte and G. Polivka, *Anmerkungen zu den Kinder- und Hausmärchen der Brüder Grimm* (Leipzig, 1912–32), 5 vols.

Elisabeth Brewer, *From Cuchulainn to Gawain, Sources and Analogues of Sir Gawain and the Green Knight* (D. S. Brewer Ltd, Cambridge, 1973).

A. Buchanan, 'The Irish Framework of Gawain and the Green Knight', in *Publications of the Modern Language Association of America*, Vol. 47, p. 315 (1932).

Ruth Crosby, 'Oral Delivery in the Middle Ages', in *Speculum*, Vol. 11 (1936).

Michael Curschmann, 'Oral Poetry in Medieval English, French and German Literature', in *Speculum*, Vol. 42 (1967).

E. E. Evans-Pritchard, *The Zande Trickster* (Oxford, 1967).

Ruth Finnegan, *Limba Stories and Story-telling* (Oxford, 1967).

Albert B. Friedman, 'Morgan le Fay in Sir Gawain and the Green Knight', in *Speculum*, Vol. 35, p. 260 (1950).

G. L. Kittredge, *A Study of Gawain and the Green Knight* (Gloucester, Mass., 1960).

A. H. Krappe, 'Who Was the Green Knight?', in *Speculum*, Vol. 13, p. 206 (1938).

R. S. Loomis, 'Gawain, Gwri, and Cuchulainn', in *Publications of the Modern Language Association of America*, Vol. 43, p. 384 (1928).

Alan M. Markman, 'The Meaning of Sir Gawain and the Green Knight', in *Publications of the Modern Language Association of America*, Vol. 72, p. 574 (1957).

William A. Nitze, 'Is the Green Knight Story a Vegetation Myth?', in *Modern Philology*, Vol. 33, p. 351 (1935–36).

Iona and Peter Opie, *The Classic Fairy Tales* (Oxford, 1974).

H. L. Savage, 'The Significance of the Hunting Scenes in Sir Gawain and the Green Knight', in *The Journal of English and Germanic Philology*, Vol. 27, p. 1 (1928).

H. L. Savage, 'The Feast of Fools in Sir Gawain and the Green Knight', in *The Journal of English and Germanic Philology*, Vol. 51, p. 537 (1952).

H. L. Savage, *The Gawain-Poet, Studies in his Personality and Background* (Chapel Hill, North Carolina, 1956).

John Speirs, 'Sir Gawain and the Green Knight', in *Scrutiny*, Vol. 16, No. 4 (1949).

Ronald A. Waldron, 'Oral-Formulaic Technique and Middle English Alliterative Poetry', in *Speculum*, Vol. 32 (1957).

J. L. Weston, *The Legend of Sir Gawain; Studies upon its Original Scope and Significance* (London, 1897).

114

B CULTURAL STUDIES

E. E. Evans-Pritchard, *Witchcraft, Oracles and Magic Among the Azande* (Oxford, 1937).
Max Gluckman, *Custom and Conflict in Africa* (Oxford, 1955).
Max Gluckman (ed.), *Essays on the Ritual of Social Relations* (Manchester, 1962).
Max Gluckman, *Order and Rebellion in Tribal Africa* (London, 1963).
Jack Goody, *The Myth of the Bagre* (Oxford, 1972).
Robin Horton and Ruth Finnegan (ed.), *Modes of Thought: essays on thinking in Western and non-Western Societies* (London, 1973).
J. Huizinga, *Homo Ludens* (Amsterdam, 1939; London, 1949).
Károly Kerényi, *The Religion of the Greeks and Romans* (London, 1962).
Marja-Liisa Swantz, *Ritual and Symbol in Transitional Zaramo Society* (Uppsala, 1970).
Victor Turner, 'Symbols in Ndembu Ritual', in *Closed Systems and Open Minds*, edited by Max Gluckman (Aldine, Chicago, 1964).
Monica Wilson, *Rituals of Kinship Among the Nyakyusa* (Oxford, 1957).

C PSYCHOLOGICAL AND PSYCHO-ANALYTICAL STUDIES

Marie Louise von Franz, *Interpretation of Fairytales* (Zurich, 1970, 1973).
Marie Louise von Franz, *The Feminine in Fairytales* (New York, 1972).
Marie Louise von Franz, *Shadow and Evil in Fairytales* (Zurich, 1974).
Roger Frétigny and André Virel, *L'Imagerie Mentale* (Geneva, 1968).
S. Freud, *Complete Psychological Works* (London, 1951 following), 24 vols.
Erich Fromm, *The Forgotten Language: an introduction to the understanding of dreams, fairy-tales and myths* (New York, 1951; London, 1952).
C. G. Jung, *Collected Works*, edited by Sir Herbert Read, Michael Fordham and Gerhard Adler (London, 1957 following), 18 vols.
C. G. Jung, *Symbols of Transformation* (1912 and London, 1952).
Carl G. Jung (ed.), *Man and his Symbols* (London, 1964).
R. D. Laing, *The Politics of the Family and other Essays* (London, 1971).
F. Riklin, *Wishfulfilment and Symbolism in Fairy Tales* (New York, 1915).
Anthony Storr, *The Dynamics of Creation* (London, 1972).

INDEX

Alice in Wonderland and *Through the Looking-Glass*, 84–5, 94

Alteration, 2–3, 7–8, 33, 53, 70, 74; elaboration, 2, 53; simplification, 2, 70

Beauty and the Beast, 84, 85

Carle off Carlile, The, 90–3

Cat-Skin, 34–9, 44, 53, 56, 58, 59, 67, 74, 84

Chaucer, *Wife of Bath's Tale*, 88, 90

Defences, 18, 31, 52, 99, 105. See also: Disguise, Rationalisation and Splitting

Disguise, 9, 12–14, 20, 25, 26, 29, 34, 38, 49, 52, 104; denial, 13–14, 27, 32, 66; displacement, 18, 31, 39, 104–5; rôle of imagery, 44–6. See also: Defences and Splitting.

Dreams, 9–16, 19

Fantasy-thinking, 9, 18, 19, 20, 25, 30, 31, 52, 55. See also: Magic.

Feelings in story: audience's recognition of, 5–6; changing, 84, 88; conflicting, 15, 27, 39, 51, 52, 58, 107; isolation of, 6, 32; in opposition to wishes, 29, 55; believed power of, 107; as source of story, 9, 10, 12, 17, 18, 20, 25, 26, 27, 31, 52, 55, 58, 59, 70, 72.

Form. See Morphology.

Frances' dream, 10–16 pass., 88

Frances' stories, 16–18

Frog Prince, The, 84, 85

Gawain and the Green Knight, Sir, 1–6 pass., 56, 74, 80–3, 96–107

Gawene and the Carle of Carelyle, Syre, 90–3

Golden Bird, The, 39–46, 53, 56, 58, 59, 67, 73, 74, 88

Hero, heroine: acknowledged, 30, 31, 32, 44, 45, 46, 62, 64, 89, 90, 92; unacknowledged, 31, 32, 44, 45, 46, 64, 92. See also: Identification

Horn, King, 59–62, 70, 74

Identification (as the key to the viewpoint), 7, 17, 20, 25, 30, 32, 38, 44, 49, 62, 84, 91–2, 93, 98, 109

Imagery, 3, 9, 15–16, 18, 26–7, 28, 31, 49, 55, 72–83, 109; conscious art's selection of, 56; rôle in disguise, 44, 46; transformation of, 85, 88

Intellectual thought in story: in creation, 18, 55, 56; in appreciation, 5–6, 56

Jane Eyre, 110

Jung, and other psychoanalysts, 8

King of the Golden Mountain, The, 20–33, 56, 58, 59, 73

Libeaus Desconus, 85–8

Magic, 1, 5, 18, 24; object, 23, 25, 29, 55, 102, 103; potion, 48, 51; sources of, 15, 27, 28, 29, 55, 84, 93, 98, 102, 104, 107; thinking, 31; word, 12, 15, 19, 28, 55, 77, 90

Marriage of Sir Gawaine, The, 88–90

Martin's dream, 11–12, 14–15, 19

Meaning: approach to, 1–7 pass., 10, 18, 20, 25, 26, 28, 30, 46, 52, 73, 78–80, 109–10; multiple significance, 15–16, 28, 32, 46, 73, 109

Morphology, 55–70; exile, 17, 25, 59, 61, 98; initial situation, 25, 28, 38, 57, 58–9, 67, 84, 91, 104; place of adventure, 25, 58–9, 67, 91, 99, 104; resolution, 45–6, 52, 58, 62, 67, 70, 84, 85, 88, 90, 93, 103–7. See also: Moves

Moves, 59, 61–70, 87, 91, 98; 104. See also: Morphology

Names in story, 49, 53, 61, 74, 83

Nonsense, 4–5

Odyssey, The, 62–70, 73, 74–80, 83

Oral tradition, 2–5

Places in story, 56–7, 79, 80

Puss-in-Boots, 84

Rationalisation, 18, 31, 56, 95

Recognition, in audiences, 5–7, 20, 25; in the hero, 85, 88, 93, 107

Red Riding-Hood, Little, 4, 6

Ritual in story, 3, 28, 31, 39, 44, 45, 56

Shape-shifting, 88. See also: Transformation

Sleeping Beauty, The, 1

Splitting, 12–13, 14, 30, 32, 44, 49; 104. See also: Disguise

Time in story, 56–7

Transformation, 84–93, 103–7

Tristan, 46–52, 54, 56, 59, 73, 74

Weddynge of Sir Gawen and Dame Ragnell, The, 88–90

Wishes: their conflicts creating story, 15, 16, 27, 29, 31, 38, 55, 58, 59, 98, 102; their opportunity in story, 6, 7

116

DATE			